# my search for love on craigslist

### By
### Michael Zinetti

*"My Search For love For Joplin! #3*
*Michael Zinetti*

**MICHAEL ZINETTI**

*Sale of this book without a front cover may be unauthorized. If this book is coverless, it may have been reported to the publisher as "unsold or destroyed" and neither the author nor the publisher may have received payment for it.*

Published by *Michael Zinetti*
Copyright 2010 by Michael Zinetti

All rights reserved under International and Pan-American Copyright Conventions. Published in the US by *Michael Zinetti*.

ISBN: 1452836418
EAN-13: 9781452836416

Manufactured in the USA

First Edition: 2010

contact info:
www.michaelzinetti.com
michaelzinetti@yahoo.com

# Dedication

This book is dedicated to...

Anyone who's ever known the pangs,
Then stole away with something sweet,
And once safe and alone,
Spied empty palms to eat.

## Some Ground Rules

Here are some self-governing ground rules: No lying or blatant misrepresentation, other than the natural tendency to embellish or contradict one's self. Must try to mention my favorite pastime: Scrabble. Must allow a week to pass between ads by the same persona, in other words, no flooding by any single persona. Additional tally rules: responses are only tallied if real. Response must mention something specific about the ad and not contain a link. Suspected spam was never counted or considered to be real, except for maybe in Emo's delusional mind.

# Michael

Michael is a penniless, out of work, and recently up-rooted goody-two-shoe man, who fancies himself a writer. To compound matters, he would like to find a hot girl with minimal expectations and a veracious love of Scrabble and movies. What better place to find a girl like that than the limitless world of Craigslist.

**1** **In Search of Scrabble and/or Movie Buddy ~ Michael's 1st Attempt**

Looking for a nice looking girl with a head on her shoulders. A girl that might get a little too competitive in a heated game of Scrabble. A girl that likes to go see movies or watch movies at home. A girl who's passionate about the things she likes. A non-smoking Christian would be ideal. Preferred age would be between 18 and 36.

**Posted: March 27, 2009 in Springfield, MO**
**Results: 7 Responses, 3 Correspondents, 0 Scrabble Games, and 0 Love**

## 2 I Guess Nobody Likes Scrabble ~ Michael's 2nd Attempt

I posted a couple weeks ago and got tons of responses but the end result was nothing. No meeting. No hanging out. And no Scrabble! What's wrong with you ladies? Is it too much to ask to find a super smart girl who can give me a run for my money in a wicked, wild game of Scrabble? And what about movies? I absolutely refuse to go see a movie by myself. I just moved back here and there's gonna be movies coming out pretty soon that I'll want to see. Are there any girls out there who want to go see *GI Joe*? Um...I guess I don't need to see that. I'm sure there are good movies coming out at some point. At which time, I'd like to have a cool girl with me, a clever sort of girl who appreciates a good movie when she sees one. Some of my favorite movies would be *One Flew Over The Cuckoo's Nest.....Reservoir Dogs......*trying to think of something more girly. It's not that I don't like chick flicks. I just don't like dumb movies - unless Will Ferrell's in them. Man, that guy is friggin' funny. I even liked him in that kids movie where he played a soccer coach. Can't remember. Anyway, I would really like these responses to go somewhere - like my bedroom. Just kidding. I don't want anyone to see my bedroom. I live with my parents. What? I said I just moved back in town. I got nothing. I don't even have a job. So, let's recap, I want a girl for Scrabbling, or going to the movies, I don't have a job, I live with my parents and I don't have much money. There, that oughta get some results. Oh, I liked *Beaches*. That's a chick flick. Right?

**Posted: April 7, 2009 in Springfield, MO**
**Results: 9 Responses, 3 Correspondents, 0 Scrabble Games, and 0 Love**

## 3 Scrabble Addict Seeks Hot Brainy Girl To Scrabble With ~ Michael's 3rd Attempt

All right, here's a slightly different approach...

First of all, if you read this and want to get it on, Scrabble-wise, please include the word HUMDINGER so I know you're not a bot.

Okay, I've been pretty successful in getting girls to respond. And some I've even passed a couple emails back and forth to. That's nice. However, in every instance, the communications have stopped there. And who knows, maybe that's my fault, cuz I'm so over-the-top obsessed with Scrabble. I like emailing and stuff, sure, but the whole point of this thing is to MEET someone. Not exchange emails and then nothing. So I'm gonna ask you Springfield ladies who like to play Scrabble to email me with the intention of playing Scrabble. This is priority one.

Just to separate the wheat from the chaff, I am not a hot, hunky dude. Surprising, huh? I am rather silly looking with several faults. Like I mentioned before, I am still unemployed and I still live with my parents. Apparently the country is in some sort of economical downward spiral, and I'm riding that spiral into abject silliness and despair. Nobody bothered to tell me before I moved back here that Springfield is apparently the cream of the crop when it comes to economic depression. Well, I'm here. And I guess I'm stuck here. So, what are we supposed to do in an economic depression? Well, play Scrabble of course.

So. Let's go. Email me. And have a pic ready or description ready. And don't be surprised when I suggest we meet for Scrabble as soon as this weekend. I want Scrabble and I want it bad. You've been forewarned. Now, email away. If you don't like Scrabble, don't bother. If you do, then I'm interested. If you're hot and you like Scrabble, I might even propose.

**Posted: April 14, 2009 in Springfield, MO**
**Results: 3 Responses, 1 Correspondent, 0 Scrabble Games, and 0 Love**

# Personae

After 3 fruitless posts, at the risk of getting bored, or perhaps to offset the pathetic and/or futile feelings coming over me, I came up with the idea to use different personae, starting with Xerx, Emo, Hub, and Davy. Xerx is a sex addict, Emo is timid and profoundly naive, Hub is the self-proclaimed gift to awesomeness, and Davy is way too honest.

# Xerx

Unlike Michael, Xerx, short for Xerxes, fears no man or anything else for that matter. Xerx possesses very little in the way of inhibitions. He is a man ruled by his desires. Xerx wears his obsession for sex and Scrabble like badges sewn to his tongue. Although this approach might make for a contemptible human being, it works wonders for making an otherwise embarrassing task of writing personals ads, well, fun.

## 4 Scrabble/Sex Addict Seeks Hot Sugar-Momma ~ Xerx's 1st Attempt

I am a super bad Scrabble/sex addict with minimal cash-flow in dire need of a hot sugar-momma for sex, Scrabble, company, and financial assistance from time to time. I have very little prospects in the arena of financial self-sufficiency but then again, neither do a lot of women reading this. I consider myself a forward thinker and am not intimidated by a woman who makes a lot of money. In fact, for the right woman, I am more than willing to sacrifice my career (which is right now just hanging out surfing the web and things like that). I realize some women will balk at the chance to support a perfectly able-bodied adult and that's fine. Lord knows I wouldn't want some hanger-on weighing me down. That is, unless that hanger-on was me.

In exchange for a safe place to rest my head and my bills paid, I will provide the following services: Scrabble whenever you want it; sex too, I guess; I will cook dinner, if you like burritos and kung pao chicken- those are the only hard things I know how to make; I will rub your back-feet-shoulder-butt as needed, I will do some cleaning, but absolutely no yard-work; I will cuddle with you for hours on end if that's the sort of person you are; I will give you one compliment a day, minimum; I will back you up when you are wrong, this caps at three times a day; I will tolerate children as long as they don't give me any lip or I feel they're threatening my peachy arrangement with you; I will accompany you shopping a maximum of 3 hours a week- I'm firm on this so use your time wisely; all other terms are negotiable.

Please email if you would like to go on a date. I like movies, music, dinner, walks, Scrabble, necking, conversation, etc. on a first date.

Please no overweight, bald, anorexic, single mothers of more than 1 kid, racist, backwards, angry women...

Please have a sense of humor, a hot body, nice legs, open mind, enabling personality, love of movies, and most of all smarts....

**Posted: May 5, 2009 in Springfield, MO**
**Results: 2 Responses, 0 Correspondents, 0 Scrabble Games, and 0 Love**

# Emo

Emo is a curious lad. He tries his very best to be even more timid and righteous than Michael, but in the end, for all his efforts, usually succeeds in dwarfing even the vilest entries by Xerx. To go along with his inadvertent brashness, Emo is surprisingly perplexed by this thing known as a computer, and even more so by this other thing, known as Craigslist. Though he is anxious to find a Godly woman, he is highly susceptible to falling into the traps set by even the most obvious predatory robot-prostitute. When faced with these menacing maidens of nothingness, Emo is oft to remind them, "I'm Christian, so don't even try it." And that, my friends, is Emo.

# 5 Would you like to meet up? ~ Emo's 1st Attempt

Hi. I'm Emo. I'm so scared about this. I would like to meet a nice girl here. Are there nice girls on here? I don't want anything to happen. I like dinner. I like movies. I like board games. My favorite is Scrabble. If anybody out there is into these things I would like to hear from you. I am Christian and I don't want any prostitutes to respond. If you are a prostitute, then please stop reading. My ideal first date is to go to a Barnes and Noble's or a library center and talk with coffee and maybe play a game, Boggle or something. I want this to be a good experience. So no prostitutes! Well, on second thought...if you are a prostitute and you want to go out, I guess it would be okay but we are absolutely not gonna do anything! We will just do the Barnes and Noble thing and we won't have absolutely any sex for money. Well, if everything goes good, and we decide to make love, I will absolutely not be willing to pay for it. I want a nice Christian girl.

**Posted: May 10, 2009 in Springfield, MO**
**Results: 2 Responses, 0 Correspondents, 0 Scrabble Games, and 0 Love**

## Greetings!

This is your author speaking. First off, I'd like to thank you so much for buying my book. Wait a minute...you did buy this book, didn't you? Oh, good. I hope you enjoy it. It won't end world hunger or cure cancer, but maybe it'll make you laugh. And in a way, doesn't laughing cure cancer little bits at a time? That's what I heard anyway.

# Hub

Hub is under the impression he's awesome. And he'd be the first one to tell you so. Admittedly, he does have a unique ability to amass a frightening amount of reasons why he's so awesome. And in some cases, the things on his lists are somewhat awesome, actually.

# **6** Awesome Guy Seeks Awesome Girl ~ Hub's 1st Attempt

I'm just wondering if there are any Hot Girls out there. If so, I'm pretty sure you're gonna want to get with me!

Here's some reasons why you should want to get with me:

-I played amateur baseball for several years
-I have my own car, a vintage 2000 Dodge Stratus
-I can bench press several, if not more, pounds
-I've been in bands and recorded a CD
-I've written two books
-I know more Chinese words than you probably know English
-I have a secret handshake
-I own several adhesives
-I can say I Love You in several languages
-I shop at Marshall's
-I have no piercings or tattoos
-I've nursed a bird back to health and taught it to fly
-I can work a VCR
-I eat everything on my plate
-I've lived all over the country
-My favorite actor is Steve Buscemi
-I graduated from MSU Magna Cum Laude
-I take risks
-I have a vast wardrobe
-I can type faster than most men
-I know more than your average person
-I've read most of the Bible
-I'm Italian
-I've driven for more than 24 hours straight
-I know how to listen
-I don't have VD
-I've written over 50 songs
-I'm not afraid of commitment
-I love America
-I own every song ever recorded by The Jam
-I believe in the socialization of medicine- Rush Limbaugh be damned
-I have connections in Branson
-I have my own phone line
-I can help you do math
-I can make kung pao chicken
-I can name every member of new kids on the block
-I invest in the stock market and don't lose money

-I own two computers but I keep one in my trunk
-I'm not afraid to get physical
-I'm not afraid to get a physical either
-I can put a scrunchy on a girl without pulling her hair
-I can drive with one hand on your lap
-I'm not afraid of Obama
-I can count to 10 in French
-I can please you in more ways than one

**Posted: May 12, 2009 in Springfield, MO**
**Results: 5 Responses, 2 Correspondents, 0 Scrabble Games, and 0 Love**

# Davy

If there were words someone on this planet should consider living by, for Davy, it would have to be the popular phrase, "too much information". Davy seems blissfully unaware of this concept.

# 7 This Probably Won't Work ~ Davy's 1ˢᵗ Attempt

I know this probably won't work but I decided to try it anyway. I know that most of these ads and the responses are fake, so I won't spend too much time on this. I'm just gonna describe myself and what I want in a girl. If you're a real girl, I'd love to hear from you. But if you're a girl hung-up on good looks and a lot of superficial stuff, than you probably should go to the next ad. I refuse to lie here, because it really is a waste of time to lie. The purpose is to find someone and get to know someone, so why would I lie? I can't hide behind fakeness forever. So I'm gonna be real. Real Honest. I am $25,000 in debt. I have no job. I collect sports cards. My favorite show is Benny Hill. I don't know anything about cars or mechanical things for that matter. I once went 7 years without having a girlfriend. I suck at reading. I sometimes go four to five days without showering. I live with my parents. I prefer that the girl drive. My favorite thing to do is play Trivial Pursuit or Scrabble. I usually don't like watching girls play sports- ie. WNBA compared to NBA, I voted for George W in 2004, I'm very cheap, I'm kind of judgmental, I have anxiety issues, my dream is to become a published author someday, and that's about it. What I want in a girl: Someone who's nice, someone who's nice to look at, someone who doesn't mind driving, someone who doesn't expect a lot from a man, someone without kids- or no more than one, someone religious- but not too religious, someone who doesn't nag, someone with long hair- I don't like girls with short hair, someone who's smart- if there's a lot of grammar issues with your response I'll assume you're not smart, someone who doesn't want to be spoiled, someone who's okay with just staying in, someone who will gladly sacrifice wining and dining for funny conversation, someone who's childish, someone who sings good, someone who doesn't laugh weird, someone who doesn't fart too much, someone who has her own hobbies but doesn't try to force them on me, someone who likes oral, someone who reads well, someone who challenges me but won't put too much pressure on me to produce, someone who doesn't mind her boobs being touched a lot, someone who doesn't watch too many stupid shows on TV, someone who likes Star Wars, someone who hates outdoorsy stuff, someone who's parents aren't overbearing or assholish, someone who inspires me, someone who likes sex, someone who is fine with going to a dollar movie, someone with a sense of humor, someone who plays Scrabble, someone who can edit a manuscript, and finally someone who can't keep their hands off me.

**Posted: May 14, 2009 in Springfield, MO**
**Results: 1 Response, 0 Correspondents, 0 Scrabble Games, and 0 Love**

# 8 Where is Joplin Anyway? ~ Michael's 4th Attempt

I get Joplin and Rolla mixed up. I know one is east and the other one is west. Are they basically the same size, population and whatnot? Anyway, I'm looking for a girl. I think I might have exhausted all the women in Springfield, at least the ones that read Craigslist. So I thought I'd try here. First off, I'm probably not in the best situation to start seeing anybody but then I thought to myself, when is? I can't seem to find a job, so I might as well look for a girl to drown my sorrows in. I just got out of a long relationship, yet another good reason not to see anybody, but again, I decided, what the heck, let's do it... I'd just like to find a girl to erase the memory of my last girl. Can girls do that? Or just alcohol? I've never really had much luck with girls from Missouri. I don't know what it is... All I want is a couple things out of a girl, good conversation, Scrabble and sex.... Is that so hard to find? Maybe in Missouri. Show me state? Show me what? Branson? Been there, done that- next.....Man this is gotta be one of the worst ads ever written. I don't even think the bots are gonna respond....

**Posted: May 15, 2009 in Joplin, MO**
**Results: 9 Responses, 3 Correspondents, 2 Scrabble Games, and 0 Love**

# 9 Would You Like To Meet (Please Humans Only)? ~ Emo's 2nd Attempt

Hi, I'm Emo. Maybe I did something wrong last time. I only want human people to respond. I got lots of responses. And I'm quite sure none of them were prostitutes. That part is good. But I'm pretty sure some of them weren't real human people. One girl, her name was MelissaXXX, said she loved my ad and she wanted me to contact her on a site she was on. So I went to the site. I made a profile. And I searched for MelissaXXX and what do you know, she didn't exist. Maybe I went to the wrong site. Two other girls, Wendy OMalley and Laurra Heintz both typed the exact same thing. They both really liiiiiiked my ad. I counted the i's. They were the same amount. But their pics were different, so I wrote to them. I told them I was a Christian and I absolutely will not date robots. Then Wendy wrote back immediately. I don't know how she responded so quickly. Anyway, she said thanks for writing and wanted me to go to a site. I felt bad so I went to the site. I made a profile. I looked up her username but she didn't exist? Weird, huh? I think Wendy and MelissaXXX are in cahoots. So, I think it's sad I have to explain this, but I simply will not enter into a relationship with a robot. I am Christian. I like women with real body parts. I especially don't like robots who are prostitutes. If you send me pictures where you are dressed in next to nothing, the first thing I will do is look at them for an hour, then I will pray for forgiveness, then I will write back, then I will look at the new pictures, then I will go to the website, then I will look at all the other pictures of robot prostitutes, then I will pray for forgiveness again, etc. So please, if it's not too much to ask. I would like a nice Christian non-robot non-prostitute girl. The things I like to do are Scrabble, movies, music, talking and being on top. If you are a prostitute, please do not respond.

**Posted: May 24, 2009 in Springfield, MO**
**Results: 6 Responses, 0 Correspondents, 0 Scrabble Games, and 0 Love**

# 10 Sex/Scrabble EXPLOSION!!! ~ Xerx's 2nd Attempt

I'm thinking of some kind of crazy Sex/Scrabble EXPLOSION! That's what's gonna happen, ladies. You hook up with me and we're gonna have a crazy unusual abnormal unwarranted beautiful Sex/Scrabble EXPLOSION! First, we'll set up the board. Then we'll decide who keeps score. You can, because I'm not good at math. Then, as we travel deeper and deeper into the wild wonderland known as Scrabble, we'll suddenly hop on each other in some kind of maddening repulsive lovely illegal harmonious fateful Sex/Scrabble EXPLOSION! If you need help with your words from time to time, I'll help you. I'm a very giving Sex/Scrabble EXPLOSION player. Maybe you're not too sure about the sex part. Or maybe you're not too sure about the Scrabble part. Well fuck you, it's gonna happen, girl! There ain't no way around it!!!! The Sex/Scrabble EXPLOSION is coming to your town! Be ready for anything!

This message brought to you by the great people at Welch's. While supplies last, you sick bitches!

**Posted: May 25, 2009 in Springfield, MO**
**Results: 2 Responses, 1 Correspondents, 0 Scrabble Games, and 0 Love**

# **B**onus **A**ttempt: In Search Of A Sancho-Like Girl ~ Michael's Attempt

I'm looking for a sancho-like girl, who's hot and filled with meat and cheese. If asked if I want her enchilada style, in other words, covered in enchilada sauce, I'll say, "No. Naked is just fine," since enchilada style would cost twice as much. While she's getting ready, I'll entertain myself with some chips and salsa. My preference is to mix one part ridiculously hot sauce, with one part medium hot sauce and one part sweet sauce, to create the most perfect multi-layered and multi-flavored salsa dip ever! When my sancho-like girl arrives, my eyes will widen and my mouth will water, or vice versa, as they always do when I see a brand new beautiful sancho lying there naked in front of me. Right away, I'll start chopping up some jalapenos and sprinkle the pieces all over her flour white skin. Then I'll smother her in my special sauce mixture. After this, chances are, she'll need to be cooled off, so I'll squirt a packet of ice-cold sour cream all over her. And now she's ready to eat. I won't waste any time. I'll dig right into her with my knife and fork, spreading and stretching her apart. I'll scoop her hot and tasty meaty innards up with some chips, savoring every bite. I won't stop until my tongue nearly bursts into flames and I have to resort to extinguishing the pain with a long sip of diet coke with lemon. When we're through, and she's got nothing left, I'll sit back in that familiar repose, and let that unexplained high come over me, as my faculties slowly return to me.

No matter how often I eat my sancho-like girl, it never gets old. It's really uncanny. Every day, this desire is renewed and my cravings start anew. One of the coolest things about my love for a sancho-like girl is she's so cheap and so easy. There's nothing, and no amount of money, keeping me from doing just that.

Oh, and I also like Scrabble.

**Never Posted For Fear Ad May Promote Cannibalism, Of Which, I Have A Zero Tolerance Policy Against.**

## 11 Looking For A Girl Who's Okay With The Following ~ Davy's 2$^{nd}$ Attempt

I believe honesty is the key to a relationship. My last post was super honest and didn't get hardly any responses. I'm gonna stick to it though, in case there's a girl out there that's into honesty. First off, I'm pretty terrible with this online dating thing. I just got out of a long relationship and I'm finding that it's having an odd effect on my behavior. I recently met a great girl on CL and scared her off because I started smothering her, sending her emails all the time. I got really crazy. I'll try not to get so crazy. I think the craziness arose when I wasn't getting ample feedback. So I may be on the needy, high maintenance side, so please take that into consideration if you intend on responding. I doubt anyone will respond but at least I got it out there. I'm just being truthful. That's the key. I'm gonna tell you a little bit about intimate things so you know exactly what you're getting yourself into. Assuming anyone will respond. Truth doesn't usually sell. So, here goes... I have an average size John Thomas but if anything it may be on the smaller side. At least this is what my last girlfriend claimed. It's not as if she was a connoisseur of cock, or maybe she was, or maybe all her ex's before me were pornstars. Regardless, this was her impression and I wanted to be truthful and share it with you. Worse than the whole size-thing is whenever I am lucky enough to find a girl willing to do things with me, I don't usually last very long. This is only in relation to intercourse and without a condom. With a condom, it's a completely different story. It lasts forever, usually because I can hardly feel anything. Without a condom, intercourse usually doesn't last more than 2 minutes. I would assume this is on account of how good it feels. Ladies, if you only knew how good it feels. However, I contend it's only because I don't get enough practice. So, ladies, if you would like to start seeing each other, and you hope to extend the 2-minute coitus, you will have to be willing to practice. You must be willing to give 110%. We may have to try it a couple times. The second or third time is always longer so there is some incentive. During oral, there is no danger of this 2-minute phenomenon. Unless you possess some sort of extraordinary powers that make you incredibly good at it. In which case, there is no guarantee to the length of time. From what I've been able to gather, for the most part, if you have a mouth, and you produce saliva, you're good at oral. As far as increasing the length of coitus, I am a true believer in practicing. So, if you respond, I will assume you won't be afraid to give it your all in this respect. I don't expect to see improvement right away. We may have to work on this several, if not more, times a week. I may be jumping the gun again, no pun intended, though, since this will hardly be a matter of issue at first. Despite my candor about this subject, I would prefer a long courtship and wouldn't expect things to progress to coitus until 3 or 4 minutes into our first meeting. Kidding, of course. I want us to take our time. I happen to think love is like a flower. It takes time to grow. And sex without love is well, really good. I meant to say, empty. And who wants empty? Probably most people. Maybe I'm old fashion but I believe that the absolute best sex happens when you're in love. Or even more so, when the couple is sexually compatible. And that's truly the point of divulging all this personal, not to mention embarrassing shit. To find someone who actually likes sex.

**Posted: May 26, 2009 in Springfield, MO**
**Results: 7 Responses, 2 Correspondents, 0 Scrabble Games, and 0 Love**

# 12 Still Awesome And Still Looking ~ Hub's 2nd Attempt

I don't understand. I listed a multitude of reasons why I'm so awesome but nothing came of it. Sure, I got some responses, but none of them were awesome.

Here's some more reasons why you want to get with me:

-I used to be in a gang
-I've never had a single broken bone in my body
-I still drive a vintage 2000 Dodge Stratus
-I smell great 60% of the time
-I'm really good with a remote control
-I'm addicted to Andy's Turtle Sundaes
-I'm a pacifist
-I'm willing to get with a girl of any race known to man, even yours
-I once jumped on top of the school roof
-I'm not so brutish I wouldn't let a woman support me if she wanted to
-I often cry several times during sappy movies
-I will defend your honor against midgets and mythical creatures
-I'm old enough to remember when MTV had music on it
-I own a 1961 Topps Mickey Mantle card worth 600 bucks
-I'm honest to a fault
-I like all kinds of food, especially if you let me eat it off your boobs
-I always put a lot of thought into my wishing well-wishes
-I always have time for grandma
-I've killed so many tiny animals in my lifetime, I will never kill again
-I can solve a Rubik's Cube in 10 minutes
-My college GPA was 3.85
-I've been known to serenade the occasional hottie
-I'm impressed with a girl who doesn't front when I ask her to go to the dollar theater with me
-I prefer it if you drive
-I've never once paid for sex
-Unless you count the whole dating process as paying for sex
-My brother can swallow an entire cheeseburger whole
-I have a phobic relationship with horseshoe crabs
-I eat sushi
-I might vote republican and then vote democrat the very next time
-My average Scrabble score is more than 350 points
-I've been known to help old ladies with their groceries and then not leave until they pay me something
-I haven't vomited in over 15 years
-My favorite thing to do with women is fondle them
-I feel the need to cover up my fart noises with clever quips, just in case

anyone's listening
-I like singing in the bathtub
-I once spent an entire evening French kissing a French girl in French speaking Quebec
-I don't scoff at people who shoot their free throws granny style
-I used to put rocks in snowballs and throw them at people
-I pissed my pants one time just to keep warm
-I've never once made a deal with the devil, not knowingly anyway
-I'm not the best example for your kids
-I can hit a ball into the corner pocket, sometimes even on purpose
-If the car ever breaks down, you'll probably have a better idea how to fix it than I will
-I'm more than willing to go for walks as long as we can stop in the woods for nooky
-When it comes to love, I'm pretty retarded
-I try to put God first, try
-I've never smoked
-I own several useless web domains
-I'm always willing to finish whatever you don't eat

**Posted: June 3, 2009 in Springfield, MO**
**Results: 10 Responses, 2 Correspondents, 0 Scrabble Games, and 0 Love**

# Truck

Truck is something of an enigma. With an insanely inept grasp of both language and art, Truck manages to mystify whoever's unfortunate enough to come across one of his ads.

# 13 Serious In Need ~ Truck's 1st Attempt

I want girl. Hot steamy girl. With big tiny boobs and hat. Four inches would be good. I make 7 dollars so I'm good. Check it. I want a girl for basic. Especially a Chinese one. Who likes. Maybe if she's good, I know. I shot the sheriff is on the radio. I like bats. A Chinese girl is good. Cooking sweet and sour good. Frivolous peanut. I'm have truck to drive if possible. Don't worry. I'm good. I speak a Chinese too like "ni hao." You do too. Please no for instance. If you do, I will be something fierce. I like a girl 5'4". Long black hair. Skinny good. Shapely good. Want left handed. Will accept right. Have stickers. Pirates are good. Astros play in Houston. Great brother. Will invest. Chinese boobs. Stir-fry cramp better. Truck it out!

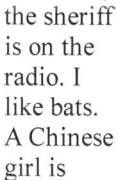

**Posted: June 6, 2009 in Springfield, MO**
**Results: Flagged and Removed, June 11, 2009**

# Bane

Bane is one picky dude. Unlike Michael, he isn't open-minded at all. He wants what he wants, and though he's not liable to get it, he tries to remain steadfast. However, at the risk of becoming a monk, something's gotta give.

# 14 Looking For The Right Girl ~ Bane's 1ˢᵗ Attempt

Hi. My name is Bane. I'm looking for the right girl. She should be short, somewhere between 5'0" and 5'5". Also, she should be skinny, so her weight shouldn't exceed 140 pounds, depending on body shape, ie. boobs. I would like her to have dark brown or black hair, at least shoulder length. I would like her to be Caucasian/Hispanic or Chinese okay. Mulatto is okay, too. I would like her to have piercing blue eyes. Must have a feminine voice and demeanor, no butchy or hoarse sounding women need apply. I would like her to have no more than 1 tattoo, preferably none. Same goes for unusual piercings. Absolutely no smokers or drug users. Must have a firm grasp of the English language. If she is ethnic, I'm willing to compromise, as long as she has some experience with the language. I would like for her to be Christian, preferably AG or Baptist. Must be willing to play around outside of marriage, ie. heavy petting and BJ's okay. Must have good taste in music and movies. I will not condone bad music, ie. country or rap (old school country and rap, okay). Likewise, I will not suffer through bad movies, ie. anything with John Cena. Must be intelligent. College GPA of 3.00 or more. No learning disabilities. Must have a job or means to support herself. Must be a legal citizen, unless Chinese, at which point I will work with this. I would like it if she is left handed, right handed okay. Please, no speech impediments, ie. stutter, stammer, or Tourette's Syndrome. Deafness okay, if so, must be patient teaching me sign language. Please no amputees or mummified people. Potential candidates should be willing to try new and different things in bed, ie. anal. Must enjoy walks or bike rides. Must enjoy board games, ie. Monopoly, chess, and/or Scrabble. She should be submissive at times, but at the same time have a backbone. Must not habitually exceed 5 miles over the speed limit. Must like Tommy Lee Jones. Must know, when I say I like Tommy Lee Jones, I'm not referring to the drummer from Motley Crue. Must not be judgmental, high maintenance, or full of expectations. Must not have high hopes. Shouldn't believe me when I say I love you, ie. when it's business time. Must not watch reality shows. Must live on the West Side of Springfield. Parents should still be together. Must not have more than 2 children, of which father of children should be completely out of the picture. On second thought, no children. Must like popcorn. Must have a serviceable singing voice. Should like to cook and clean. Must not nag. Should be creative. Must be patient. Must enjoy being touched at any time, ie. breasts, in supermarket. Must not use the expression, "Rock on" or "That's sick." Must have an inny, ie. not an outy. Must enjoy conversation. Must be willing to procreate, eventually.

**Posted: June 7, 2009 in Springfield, MO**
**Results: 1 Response, 0 Correspondents, 0 Scrabble Games, and 0 Love**

## 15 Any Scrabble Lovers In Springfield ~ Michael's 5th Attempt

Hey, just wondering if there are any Scrabble lovers in Springfield. I'm not gonna talk about love or sex or my awful station in life. I'm just gonna get down to the bare bones of it, the brass tax of it, and say I'm looking for a girl who loves Scrabble. I've been unequally yoked in the past and I wanna steer clear of that. Meaning, I've dated women in the past who didn't like Scrabble, and let me tell you, it's hard. It's unnecessarily hard. In all honesty, Scrabble is my thing. You might have your thing. And I would hope I would be good at whatever that is, but my thing is Scrabble. I don't want to pussy-foot around it anymore. Basically, you must either love Scrabble or at least have acumen for the game, and be willing to play. I would love it all the more, if you had a passion for it. I'm sure I can't expect you to love it as much as me, but something close would be nice. I have other interests and things I'd like out of a girl, but why go on if this simple thing isn't met. I know I must sound cold. I'm not a cold person. I guess I'm a little jaded by this whole process. So, if you will, take mercy on me, and be honest about the Scrabble thing. The movie watching, book reading, coffee drinking, dinner eating, church going, sex having, can all come later. Scrabble first, then sex. That should be a general rule with me. Thanks for reading and sure hope this works...

**Posted: June 17, 2009 in Springfield, MO**
**Results: 9 Response, 5 Correspondents, 2 Scrabble Games, and 0 Love**

# 16 Where Are You, MelissaXXX? ~ Emo's 3rd Attempt

Dear beautiful robot-prostitute. I'm Emo. You wrote me a while ago. You said you liked my post and wanted to meet, but you were worried I might kidnap, tie you up, and keep you there until you peed yourself. Well, I can understand your concern. I mean, if anyone is out there looking to tie up a girl until she pees herself, he's probably on Craigslist. You wanted to make sure you would be safe so you asked me to go to your site, bighotbootyliciouschickswithdicks.com. So, just so we both felt safe, I went to bighotbootyliciouschickswithdicks.com and made a profile. After I filled out all my personal information, like my name, address, social security number and my credit card number, including the 3-digit code on the back, I looked around for your profile. But you were nowhere to be found. After a while, I had to give up. I'm not an idiot. I know you're a robot-prostitute. And you've had a hard robot-prostitute life. After some contemplation, and a bit of praying, I decided all that stuff didn't matter. If two people love each other, or if one person and one robot-prostitute love each other, then there is nothing in this world that can stop them. So please, MelissaXXX, if you're out there, please find this ad, for the sake of our future half-human/half-robot children. Your Emo.

**Posted: June 21, 2009 in Springfield, MO, in Missed Connection Section**
**Results: 0 Responses, 0 Correspondents, 0 Scrabble Games, and 0 Love**

# 17 Hooters/Scrabble Fantasy ~ Xerx's 3rd Attempt

Oh, yeah. I'm looking for a girl to play a sweet and dirty game of Scrabble. Ideally, she should be dressed similarly to a Hooters girl. Yeah, a wicked smart Hooters girl who's really good at Scrabble. It could happen. The Hooters girl should actually look like a Hooters girl. And if possible, act like one, too. You know, flirtatious, and yet possess a clear and present set of boundaries. She might call you "hun" or "babe" and stick her boobs in your face, but she should totally object to anything like sitting on your lap or something like that. It really is an irresistible dichotomy. Boobs are a must. I repeat, ideal candidate must have boobs. Big ones are a plus but any size boobs are acceptable, as long as they're on display for all the world to see, behind an extremely tight shirt or tank top. I'm flexible with the Scrabble thing. Of course, I would prefer a girl who averages 350 points a game, but will settle for a girl who can't even count to 7 without using her fingers. I can't wait to get started! This is gonna be so hot and crazy, I might cry. Oh, that reminds me: ideal candidate shouldn't be turned off by men who cry during sex.

**Posted: June 25, 2009 in Springfield, MO, in Casual Encounters**
**Results: 0 Response, 0 Correspondents, 0 Scrabble Games, and 0 Love**

# 18 A Nice Christian Nymphomaniac Girl... ~ Davy's 3rd Attempt

As worthless as honesty apparently is, I'm gonna continue with this fruitless approach. As I get older, I'm beginning to value a relationship with God. Perhaps, this is because, as time goes by, and with every passing life, I'm reminded of my own mortality. So, as if things weren't hard enough with CL, I'm about to make it even harder. I would like to emphasize I want a Christian girl. Now, I'm not the best Christian in the world, and so, I wouldn't expect to find or win over a Super Christiany girl. In all honesty, some people are a little too Christiany, and when we're talking about finding a potential mate, that's a potential turn off. Sure, I guess, it would be nice to have a Super Christian girl to keep me on the straight and narrow. But in the end, that's really up to me. Besides, I already have a woman who nags me about my walk with Jesus, and that position belongs to my Mom. I don't need another one of those. What I do need, however, is a nice girl with a Christian foundation. If she listens to her Amy Winehouse, or swears from time to time, or smokes, I'll be honest, that stuff will probably grate on my nerves, but like I said, I'm not the best Christian in the world. And I too, dig on the Amy Winehouse. With that said, I would be more than a little impressed with a girl that is a devoted Christian, but also has a ferocious appetite in bed. I think, that's what a lot of men want, and I guess I'm no different. I would love a girl that is all churchy, but then, when we're sitting on the couch watching a movie, she might grab my willie and not let go til I'm coming like crazy all over God's creation. This works well with one of my other posts, where I expressed some concern about my lackluster sexual prowess. I insisted whoever answers my ad, must be willing to give 110% in bed and practice several times a week. Otherwise, things might never get better. And I still stand by that. But now, I would like to add that this girl, this most charitable and generous and amorous girl, must be Christian. Or at least have some sort of religious grounding. This'll make the sex that much wronger. So wrong it'll be right. Ultimately, in terms of the future, I can't think of a better recipe for a long and loving marriage than church 2-3 times a week, mixed in with a whole lotta dirty, crazy, nasty, organismic sex. Can you?

**Posted: June 30, 2009 in Springfield, MO**
**Results: 7 Response, 3 Correspondents, 2 Scrabble Games, and 0 Love**

# 19 Girl Boobs (Chinese) ~ Truck's 2nd Attempt

I recently hat on boobs and I was in love. Porcupine no way! Fourteen days until Christmas and I was Henry. Real name the Truck. Funny huh? I'm in search of a girl with boobs. I like need and will care for a girl with boobs. Derek Jeter just hit a homey. I'm trying to be honest. And a hat on her boobs is impressive. Like dancers in a show place. I want a girl for basic. Chinese is good but Mandarin is better. Ni hao. Ni you mei you boobs? Da xiao da da boobs? Hecklers are decent. Long hair is good. Shapely good. Trident gum stings my tongue but names will never hurt me. Madonna is one adopting fool! Hurray for Hollywood? What are we? Prince and the Revolution. Notorious. Frivolous Peanut. Crying Game has one weird ending! Impressive Hat Trick! Frappes the drink not the dance move! Priscilla Presley. Chinese big tiny boob. Truck it out!

**Posted: July 2, 2009 in Springfield, MO**
**Results: Flagged and Removed, July 3, 2009**

# Truck Dilemma

I was afraid of this. It turns out the world isn't quite ready for Truck. After two God-awful attempts in which he spilled out his guts for all of Missouri to see, he was viciously flagged and removed. I'm not completely unfeeling. As appalled as I may be, too, by Truck, he is still my creation. So I will no longer permit him to cast his moronic pearls before swine. Truck is returning from whence he came. Back to the abyss affectionately referred to as my mind. Perhaps never to be seen again. Truck it!

# 20 More Reasons Why I'm Awesome... ~ Hub's 3rd Attempt

I got a good response last time but she wasn't quite awesome enough. You need to be awesome if you're gonna try to get with me. I mean it. If you can't honestly look in the mirror and tell yourself you're awesome, than how do you expect me to tell you you're awesome? So do yourself a favor and make sure you're awesome before you email me.

More reasons why I'm so awesome...

-I can pray and God listens, I'm sure
-I can get 3 strikes in a row when I'm bowling
-I can also get 3 strikes in a row when I'm batting
-I don't hunt
-I make a lot of ill-conceived promises
-I can kiss you without slobbering
-I like sports
-I wrote a song last night about how love is a mother-fucker
-I've had several get rich schemes, and thus far, they've all conspired to keep me poor, the worst of which being college
-I will hold you so tight, it's stupid
-I fall in love an average of 5 times a year
-I know the Dewey Decimal System, or at least I know of it
-I was very saddened by Michael Jackson's passing
-I have no problem telling a girl she has eyes like Bob Dylan, as it is a compliment, dumbass!
-I'm not so old-fashion I won't let a girl pay for dinner
-I wear a size 3X even though I could wear a size 2X
-On a related note, I love sanchos
-I can drive but I'm not too happy about it
-I cry late at night
-I write books
-I can't whistle very good
-I tend to give people the benefit of the doubt
-Everyday is a bad hair day for me
-I'm willing to drive really far for love
-I've never once flicked off a clergyman
-I have no problem waiting to open presents
-I own an autographed Juan Marichal card.
-I break down carbon atoms
-I think I know how to find your g-spot
-I graduated high school in 1993
-In theory, I procreate
-I used to have sex everywhere, and in all the wrong places

-I prance around in my undies
-I hate commercials
-I can lift any girl below 120 pounds
-I know the squareroot of 139
-I hate housework and yardwork equally
-I have an irrational fear of flying
-I voted for Ralph Nader
-I can beat girls at anything, apart from vaginally related contests
-I can tolerate most children and pets
-On a related note, I believe in corporal punishment
-I know some of my rights
-I'm way better than you at Scrabble
-Sometimes, when the mood strikes and the planets align just right, I can get to third base with myself
-I know about 300 Chinese words
-I never believed in Santa Claus
-I love Benny Hill
-The more I like you, the more I obsess
-I forget how to do math
-I still like Mel Gibson and always will
-I don't discriminate, I'm equally afraid of everyone
-I like to be touched
-I avoid some traffic circles
-I love Hooters, both the restaurant and the body part that inspired it
-I wish I had a tolerable career
-If we ever play strip poker, you better dress in layers
-I can play a Bm chord without looking
-I can also have a bm without looking
-I sing whenever I want

**Posted: July 9, 2009 in Springfield, MO**
**Results: 2 Responses, 1 Correspondent, 0 Scrabble Games, and 0 Love**

# 21 Revised Wants And Needs ~ Bane's 2nd Attempt

Hi. I'm Bane. I would like to try this again. Last time, I might have been a little picky- as is my nature. I will try to be more flexible this time around. I'm looking for the right girl. Must have boobs. Preferable 2. Must enjoy Duran Duran. Must not be habitually sarcastic. I originally said I wanted either a Caucasian, Hispanic, or Asian. I'm now expanding this to include Indian, on account of that very hot chick from *Slumdog Millionaire*. The girl I need must be flexible, ie. not have a hissy if I do things like leave the toilet seat up or try to find her sister's g-spot. The ideal girl shouldn't be judgmental or critical, ie. I can't parallel park to save my life. She shouldn't wear any clothes with cartoon characters on them. The girl should be intelligent, ie. must know the socialization of medicine and healthcare is a no-brainer most of the civilized world has already figured out. Must be malleable. Must be shapely, curvaceous, ie. look like a girl, meaning, shouldn't look like a twelve year old boy or shaped like a pear. The ideal girl shouldn't still have a crush on actors like Tom Cruise or that ultra hot doofus from the *Twilight* movies. Oh, that reminds me, shouldn't like *Twilight* or *Harry Potter*. Must know who Henry James and William Faulkner are. Must be willing to do things to me all the time, and vice versa. Can't want to rescue stray animals all the time. Mustn't pick at her salad like a bird. Needs to have long dark hair. Must not be tattooed to the point of idiocy. Must be willing to jaywalk. That reminds me, must like Letterman over Conan or whoever. I have to find a girl who enjoys sports and shares a passion for vegging out with a nice Yankees/Red Sox game. Must know who Don Mattingly is. Can't be cynical about death. Must like the books and songs I write. If not, must be either willing to keep an open mind, or lie if needbe, when asked if she likes my books or music. Ideal candidate should welcome random middle-of-the-night sex. Perfect girl should have a healthy relationship with God and a clear understanding about what it means to be a Christian. No atheists or Wiccans need apply. Unless they're really hot, in which case I will gladly lose my soul for some serious nooky. Can't enjoy public displays of farting or burping. Must be cool with wearing skirts or dresses, as these are simply the most exciting and sexy things women wear, not only for their easy access qualities, but also for their ability to universally beautify the female frame. Speaking of frame, she can't be taller than me, preferably in the 5'0 to 5'6 range. Will consider shorter but not taller. Must have a healthy personality and sense of humor. Must enjoy sex in cars. Must not ask me if I'd like to play Skip-Bo or Phase 10, opting instead for Scrabble or Boggle or oral sex. Must enjoy spooning. Must be willing to drive. No flirting with other men, in fact, must be repulsed by all other men, even Tom Cruise or that bum-licker from *Twilight*. Must enjoy Benny Hill.

**Posted: July 18, 2009 in Springfield, MO**
**Results: 1 Response, 0 Correspondents, 0 Scrabble Games, and 0 Love**

## 22 Wanna Go To The Movies? ~ Michael's 6th Attempt

Hello, Springfield women and bots alike. Is anyone out there interested in going to see a movie in the next few nights? I promise I won't put the moves on you. I absolutely, under any circumstances will not pretend to yawn and then next thing you know, I'm all over you like white on rice. There's a movie I'd like to see before it leaves the theaters and I think the most depressing thing on the planet is to go see movies by yourself. It's almost as depressing as looking for love on Craigslist. Well, this isn't love. This is me trying to find a girl willing to go see a movie with me. If you are interested please send me an email and pic. That'd be nice. I won't include a pic because I'm old and ugly. If you wanna skip the whole pic thing, I'll just assume you're ugly too, in which case, it doesn't really matter since all I wanna do is go see a movie together. If we should meet and fall in love, that's okay too. But mainly, I'm trying to get that movie thing happening. If you send a pic, I'll do the same, out of courtesy and plus it'll give me a chance to say I told you so, concerning the whole old and ugly thing. I'm not the sort of person who lives to tell people I told you so, but it is fun to say from time to time.

Some other things of interest... I like going to church (most of the time), I like music, I like movies (obviously), and I suck at Scrabble. Presently, I haven't yet given up on Barack Obama. Nor do I think he's the antichrist like most people around here seem to think- ie. the people at my church (perhaps this would be reason #1 why I don't like going to church).

**Posted: August 3, 2009 in Springfield, MO**
**Results: 5 Responses, 4 Correspondents, 3 Movies, and 0 Love**

## 23 Seriously Loosening Up On Qualifications ~ Bane's 3rd Attempt

Hi. I'm Bane. It has been well over a month since my last post. I got next to nil for responses and so something's gotta give. In this case, I will do just that. Give. So now, all I require is the girl is hot. Tattoos and piercings okay, as long as they don't cause me to projectile vomit when I see them. Must not pee standing up. Must be either Caucasian, Hispanic, Asian, Asian Indian, and now accepting African American. Must have a tolerance toward all the weird things I like, ie. pistachios, Scrabble, Benny Hill, handjobs, etc.. Can't assault me whenever she wants, unless sexual, in which case that's fine. No forming clusterfucks. Must be appreciative when I slave away for a whole hour making her burritos. After eating the burritos, must fart in a discreet fashion, not in front or behind or on me. No titty twisters. Must be pleasant. Must be compassionate when I get whiny. Has to think the war in Iraq and Afghanistan is silliness. Must have a body with 2 boobs - this is non-negotiable. Augmented boobs okay. Must be honest. Must have a propensity for swallowing. Can't get excited when hunky men are on TV. Must welcome my inopportune and badly timed advances, ie: at funerals. Must be willing to visit me in the bathtub. Isn't allowed to make fun of me when I sing to my favorite music while in the bathtub. Must enjoy going to movies. Must be okay with me touching boobage in almost every setting. Can't be able to fight this feeling anymore. Must not think the lead singer of REO Speedwagon is dorky, even if it's obvious he is. Must have a nice singing voice. Must enjoy conversation. I said before she must be 5'0 to 5'6 range. I'm willing to expand this range to 4'8 to 5'6. Income not important, referring to mine. Must be willing to kiss me the very second we see each other. Dark features are preferred. No incessant swearing. Must appear virginal and yet slutty at the same time. Needs to cover up the merchandise. Must be willing to watch Idol with me and my family. Kids okay. Must have low expectations in almost every way. Must enjoy driving. Prefer a girl who doesn't cut. Must not have strange laugh. No protruding teeth or overbites. Must be willing to be on top.

**Posted: September 3, 2009 in Springfield, MO**
**Results: 5 Responses, 2 Correspondents, 0 Scrabble Games, and 0 Love**

## 24 Scrabble/G-Spot Adventure Party ~ Xerx's 4th Attempt

I'd like to go on an adventure. I'm picturing Scrabble; lots of hot and heavy, naughty Scrabble. Mixed in with a dirty game of Scrabble, I imagine, there will be numerous perilous expeditions, southward, into the deep of your most happiest place. I don't know, how 'bout whenever I score a 40-point word or higher, I'm afforded the opportunity to grab some lubricant and whatnot and reach down around your nether region, as deep as my fingers will allow, in search of that ever elusive G-Spot. Once found, I'm sure we will reap untold riches, far beyond our wildest dreams. The ideal candidate for this adventure should have a good sense of direction. Must not fold under pressure. And perhaps more important than those requirements, she must be willing to reciprocate. I repeat, must be willing to reciprocate. Looking like a Hooters girl would be a definite plus. However, in these desperate times, any nice looking, honest, kind-hearted, sweet, happy-go-lucky, funny, down-to-earth, nymphomaniac will more than fit the bill.

**Posted: September 3, 2009 in Springfield, MO**
**Results: 0 Responses, 0 Correspondents, 0 Scrabble Games, and 0 Love**

## 25 Life After MelissaXXX ~ Emo's 4th Attempt

I'm emo. After my heart was broken, I am no longer open to a relationship with a robot-prostitute. I realize a relationship is best if both people are humans. So, if there are any nice Christian women who would like to have premarital sex, please write me. However, if we were to have sex, I absolutely will not pay for it, so don't try to charge me or send me a bill in the mail. I will not pay it. I am Christian, so don't even try it. If you are a robot-prostitute please show some compassion and refrain from writing me. I'm weak. I've been looking at internet porn for several hours straight and if I get anymore, I might be forced to do something drastic. I like walking on beaches, eating at Andy's, slimy wet kisses, and certain smells. Please talk to me. I'm right here. I'm not a robot, so don't treat me like one. Emo out.

**Posted: September 3, 2009 in Springfield, MO**
**Results: 2 Responses, 1 Correspondent, 0 Scrabble Games, and 0 Love**

# 26 Looking For A Girl To... ~ Xerx's 5th Attempt

Looking for a nice girl to put my penis inside. I will put it in there. Or there. Or even there. I will. Please respond soon. Time is of the essence. Must be willing to play Scrabble before or after or both. In some cases during. It will take a special girl to do this.

I thought about putting this ad in the no strings attached section but thought better of it. I realize now the girl I'm looking for is probably one in a million. So I imagine I will like to hold onto whoever is okay with all this.

I'm very cautious about who I have sex with, so I will need a minimum of 40 minutes to get to know you first. If I feel as though you are the right girl for the job, we will enter the Scrabble portion of the date. If you prove yourself to be a good Scrabble player/or exhibit any amount of potential, chances are, if all goes well, and the planets align, I will put my penis inside you. If memory serves me right, this will feel really good. I will put it in there for as long as you permit me to. However, it has been a long time so I imagine it won't exceed 10 minutes. At which point, we can play another game of Scrabble or watch a movie or just talk about life. When approximately 30 minutes has passed, I will probably like to put my penis inside you again. If you are a good sport, you will comply. In theory, the second time will be a lot longer. Perhaps 15 minutes. If need be, foreplay and other board games can be used to extend the sexual portion of the date.

The next portion is the not wanting to leave portion of the date. I will probably not want to leave. Especially if you are super good looking. I might even propose. At which point, you will need to figure out a smooth way of letting me down. A good way to do this is to simply offer to let me put my penis inside you one more time. Depending on how it goes, I might forget about the whole proposing thing, as I tend to forget a lot of things when my penis is inside there. However, in some rare cases, you may actually want to proceed to the marriage portion of the date. Please, if you agree to this, you must understand, we will forever be locked in a sort of Scrabble/penis-inside-you rut from here to eternity. Sure we'll have lots of fun, talking, joking around, watching movies, hanging out, being best friends, but ultimately, it will always boil down to the Scrabble/penis-inside-you thing.

Thank you

**Posted: September 13, 2009 in Springfield, MO**
**Results: 5 Responses, 4 Correspondents, 2 Scrabble Games, and 0 Love**

## 27 You Want Me So Bad It Hurts! ~ Hub's 4th Attempt

I'm trying not to be so awesome in this post. I think my other posts might have painted a picture too grandiose and thus unattainable for the mere mortal woman. I am simply trying to describe myself. Is it my fault I'm so awesome? Unlike previous posts, I communicated that I would like an equally awesome girl to be with. Well, in all honesty, I fear that may not be possible. So I would simply just like a girl to respond. Any girl will due. As long as she's cool with the fact that I'm so awesome.

More reasons why I'm awcsome:

-I like *Spiderman*
-I speak to God on a regular basis
-No matter how sick I get, I never die
-I just made 100 dollars on the stock market
-I will squeeze you so hard you'll pop
-I'm not hung up on name brands
-I can eat a taco and drive at the same time
-I recently collaborated on a song about the sunshine of my cunt, even when I don't have one
-I can tell you I love you in Chinese
-I support Obama
-I'm currently writing a novel
-I've gone to 3 different churches in the last 3 weeks
-I could eat a sancho every day if I wanted to
-I like Letterman over Leno/Conan
-I will find your g-spot
-I can drive a car and not get us killed
-On a related note, I was moved by Ted Kennedy's funeral on C-span
-I think Kanye West is a big baby
-I can write a song about you in 5 minutes flat
-I only watch an hour of TV a day, if that
-I recently reached the 6 month mark without a job
-I honor most of the 10 Commandments
-I like boobs in my face
-I have an aversion to manual labor
-I can talk on the phone more than 2 hours at a time
-I snore so loud I wake myself up sometimes
-I might fondle you on our very first date
-I just lost 100 dollars on the stock market
-I like pooping
-I will never use the words twat, douche, or cunt
-I can put my entire John Thomas inside you

-I think Ellen will do an okay job
-I will never ever do that again, not until the next time
-I have a blog
-I recently fell flat on my butt
-I can smell good
-You want me so bad it hurts
-If you Scrabble, you have a very good chance of winning me over

**Posted: September 15, 2009 in Springfield, MO**
**Results: 4 Responses, 2 Correspondents, 0 Scrabble Games, and 0 Love**

## 28 Who Wants To Cuddle? ~ Davy's 4th Attempt

Okay, now I'm just getting silly. Sure, I'd still like a nice Christian nymphomaniac girl, but I realize Christian nymphomaniac girls don't grow on trees. So now, basically, all I'm asking from the greater Springfield area is a nice girl to cuddle with. I know cuddling sounds sissy-ish. And I'm sure there isn't a woman out there that dreams about a man who likes to cuddle. Cuz God knows I can't do much else. I can't fix your car, I can't fix your house, I can't wine and dine you, I can't do much, but what I can do is cuddle the mess out of you. I can hold you and squeeze you and maybe make you laugh or play Scrabble with you, but that's about it.

A long time ago, I had a girlfriend. You guys should have been there. It was great. Late at night, I would be doing stupid stuff on the computer, writing a book or whatnot, and then I'd go to bed. My girlfriend would already be asleep. Then I would get into bed and wrap my arms around her and, well, cuddle. It was nice. She might wake up and give me a kiss. That's nice. It's kind of hard to sleep while cuddling, so eventually I'd let her go and turn over and start sawing logs.

I realize nobody likes the idea of being a replacement. It's not good for ones ego, I guess. I know all of you would decline if I were to say, "Looking for a girl to replace my ex-girlfriend". So let me state clearly, our cuddling, yours and mine, would be a completely new and different animal. I wouldn't once, accidentally call out my ex-girlfriend's name while we were in repose. Yeah. Just a nice drowsy sort of game of Twister without the Twister.

**Posted: September 17, 2009 in Springfield, MO**
**Results: 3 Responses, 1 Correspondent, 0 Scrabble Games, and 0 Love**

## 29 In Need Of Girl With 2 Boobs ~ Bane's 4th Attempt

I'm in need of girl with 2 boobs. Preferably a pretty face and hot body should surround the 2 boobs. The color of body isn't important: red, white, blue, red again, black, brown, paisley, etc. Must be willing to reach into my pants at the drop of a hat. A college degree isn't required, but preferred. Must not have more than 2 kids. Height requirements are 4'0 to 5'8. Weight must not exceed 200 pounds, due to my tendency to lift girls up and carry them off to bed. I'm pretty firm on these specifications. Looking for a girl for basic. Cleanliness important. Must have an ample sense of humor. Ambidextrous girls may be given priority over non-ambidextrous girls, as it pertains to ease in which to grab my Johnson at any angle. Must own either a Smiths, Rufus Wainwright, Bob Marley, Motown, Jam, Alison Krauss, or Radiohead CD. Must be willing to endure the taste of cum every now and again and again. Would like a girl for church. Excessive swearing may get you tied up and mistreated for several hours. Must be willing to drive. Can't fart or belch like a pirate. No foaming at the mouth. Rudeness, like checking your phone every five seconds, will not be tolerated. Must support healthcare reform. Must not be living with, still seeing, or thinking fondly of ex-boyfriend all the time. Must be willing to go to Hooters, and/or dress up like a Hooters girl every now and then. No visible tattoos of ex-beaus' names. Tramp stamp okay, as long as it's not a distracting image, ie. my mom, your mom, jesus, or conjoined twins. No taking me shopping. No excessive use of overused pop-culture phrases like "right on" or "that's sick". Materialistic girls need not apply. No going through my stuff.

**Posted: September 19, 2009 in Springfield, MO**
**Results: Flagged and Removed, September 20, 2009**
**Reposted: September 20, Manhattan, NY**
**Results: 1 Response, 1 Correspondent, 0 Scrabble Games, and 0 Love**

# 30 Looking For Model ~ Michael's 7th Attempt

I'm looking for a cute girl to model for me. Will pay $10 for signed release of photos. In some cases, I may develop a crush. If I should do that, please be advised, our modeling relationship may be altered accordingly. If at some point, you start to feel uncomfortable, for instance, if I ask you to take your shirt off, or in some cases I take my shirt off, please feel free to state your feelings. Speak slowly and clearly in a direct manner, otherwise, I may be too enamored to process what you're saying. After the photo shoot, if, by chance, I start sending you silly emails, where I profess my love, I would suggest you move that email, and those that follow, to your spam folder. In the unlikely event you are receptive to these advances, a relationship will more than likely ensue. At which point I will more than likely love you forever. Must provide ID. If you should have any questions regarding the purpose of these photos, don't hesitate to ask. Those interested are asked to send an email with attached photo(s). Thank you and I hope to hear from you soon.

**Posted: September 19, 2009 in Springfield, MO, in Talent Gigs**
**Results: 3 Responses, 2 Correspondents, 1 Photo Shoot, and 0 Love**
    **Flagged and Removed, September 21, 2009**

# Rome

Rome is pretty much the world's worst poet. He is sort of a manifestation of this incredibly bad poet I saw in this campy, and completely unwatchable movie called *Hollywood Zap!* Rome, is, however, completely unaware he is so awful. In fact, he thinks he's quite good. Unfortunately, nobody else would think so.

## 31  To My Sweet Craigslist Princess (Or Something Like That) ~ Rome's 1st Attempt

To My Sweet Craigslist Princess or something like that
With all the like stuff I always wished I had
Like something super sort of sweet
Or like a flowery garden trick or treat

Kept hidden in your big hairy bush
Where within many a lonely knight was mistook
And I see your hot sculpted hair
Where upon you have lots of product there

> Like totally like a valley girl
> Like a lion's thick mane?
> Like Nikki Sixx, you know, from that 80's glam band?

I spy your burning red eyes
From when you start to sweat and product seeps into your eyes
And in the dark glow your really good teeth
Like something super white or like neat

I anticipate our first meeting with great anticipation
We will be like so happy
You will grab at me and I will grab at you

> Like trigger-happy cats
> Like kleptomaniacs
> Like bags full of crap or something like that

And you with all of the good things you got
And me like so big and like hard as a rock
We will mash meat between the sheets
And mix up juices like party punch solution
And when all is said and done
We will come

> Like all ye faithful
> Like the sprinklers outside my window at night
> Like an earthquake you feel with a whole bunch of delight

Because you are my sweet Craigslist Princess
And I your chivalrous knight, Sir Rome

**Posted: October 12, 2009 in Springfield, MO**
**Results: 1 Response, 1 Correspondent, 0 Scrabble Games, and 0 Love**

## 32 Church Girl Needed For Mexican Food ~ Emo's 5th Attempt

I have to wash my hands. Like Pancho Pilot. No more noodling for nooky. No more messing around with Robot-Prostitutes. They leave you empty inside. And in the end, break your heart. I am Emo, hear me roar. I will accept no sugar substitute. I feel empowered. I would really like to have a nice Christian girl with formidable knockers and a veracious appetite for sex. Must be actual authentic Christian. In other words, doesn't attend a silly church with a name like sunshiny togetherness happy anything-goes spiritual life no-consequences center. For some unknown reason, Emo loves Mexican Villa. We will meet there. I will order a sancho and mix the hot, mild, and sweet sauces together and eat it. You will be there, too. I might play footsies with you and then again I might not. Please don't get between Emo and his sancho. If you do, Emo isn't responsible for what happens. Then a movie at the cheap theater. Then a coffee at a place. Maybe a game of Scrabble or Boggle. No prostitution at any time, please. Don't try to trick me. I am Christian so I know when someone is being prostitute-like. You will lose! If at anytime throughout the date, we are abducted by aliens or robot beings, I will try my best to protect you. But no promises. If, for some reason, we are separated on the alien ship, let's try to meet back at Mexican Villa. Just to be on the safe side, in the beginning of the date, I will more than likely ask you to sign a release form stating that Emo isn't responsible for your safety if we are abducted by aliens or robot beings. Refusal to sign the release may result in immediate termination of our date. At which time, you will be expected to give me a French kiss and bid me a fond farewell. Heaven help us. Hallowed be thy name. Amen. Emo out.

**Posted: October 19, 2009 in Springfield, MO**
**Results: 4 Responses, 2 Correspondents, 1 Sancho, and 0 Love**

# 33 Still Looking And Yet Not Finding The Perfect Girl ~ Bane's 5th Attempt

Why is it that nobody ever responds to my ads? I'm merely explaining what I want. Isn't that what this whole thing is about? So here goes....

Hi. I'm Bane. I'm looking for a girl who's 4' to 5'10. Must shave. Race is not an issue. No more than 3 tattoos. No membership in any cults, AG okay. Some weirdness okay. Must enjoy sex. Must be smart but not too smart, ie. mental telepathy a no-no. No juggling required. No excessive smacking of my butt. Must be employed. No more than 2 kids. Must not be currently living with or still doing ex-boyfriend. No reality shows. Minimal swearing allowed. Preferably no smoking. No exposition of bodily functions, ie. no bathrooming with door wide open, no belching or farting or howling at the moon - unless you're a werewolf. If you're a werewolf, absolutely no biting. Unless biting will grant me eternal life. However, I don't imagine turning into a werewolf is very comfortable - in fact, after seeing various werewolf movies it looks quite painful. Then again, eternal life sounds good. That's more along the lines of a vampire. In which case, if you are a vampire, you must not suck my blood in excess of 5 ounces a day. Beyond that, I might become light-headed and/or pass out while driving. If at any time, I happen to pass out, optimal way to wake up is finding my Johnson in your mouth - a surprising and fun way to wake up in almost any circumstance. What was I talking about? Oh yeah, preferably, I'd like a girl who enjoys flashing me, and not so much flashing coworkers or passersby. Must be willing to consider working the word "awesome" into her vocabulary. Must not listen to death metal or any other music with unintelligible screaming- unless it's punk, which is kind of cute at times, ie. Chaotic Dischord. No ultra crazy fanatical Christians need apply. However, some Christian morals are essential. Ideally, candidate should possess a great deal of creativity, which she might express through poetry, music, art, or writing. Please, no white supremacists. Knowledge of kung-fu not important, but appreciated. Knowledge in anything, really, is appreciated. No girls with over 20 past lovers need apply. No haters of word games like Boggle or Scrabble need apply. Must enjoy fondling and being fondled. No materialistic women need apply, ie. must not insist on diamonds, especially after seeing *Blood Diamond*. No shape-shifters, especially if shape-shifting is spontaneous and/or involuntary - that'd get annoying. Must enjoy or at least be willing to pretend to enjoy sushi.

**Posted: October 22, 2009 in Springfield, MO**
**Results: 3 Responses, 2 Correspondents, 0 Scrabble Games, and 0 Love**

# Petur

Petur likes to tell tall tales. He is the only persona to be given poetic license to write whatever he feels. He especially likes to come up with his own out-there personas or scenarios. However, no matter how out-there his stuff is, it is always, as it was on Craigslist, preceded by the disclaimer: "The Following Is Made Up."

## 34 Famous Cowboy In Town For One Night Only ~ Petur's 1st Attempt

The following is made up....

Hello, all you gorgeous ladies of Springfield. I just flew in today and I'm doing a show at a local bar and then the rest of my night is free. I'll be on my way to Branson shortly thereafter, so I won't be in Springfield long. Just one night. Still, while I was here, I was hoping to meet a nice Show-Me State girl. If possible a girl that sums up the region. After cruising around in my limo, I can probably piece together what a typical Springfield girl should be like...I can pretty much bet she goes to one of them great big churches. Am I right? That is, when she isn't stopping by the nearest Brown Derby or Mexican Villa. I'm on Campbell now and I think it's safe to assume, she probably goes to buffets and more than likely has a bit of a weight problem. I'm guessing she probably goes to a college that meets in a converted department store. To make ends meet, she nurses at one of the hospitals. Then, for extra cash, probably strips off her uniform at one of the strip joints on Glenstone. She might listen to country music- which works out nicely for me. And she probably has some kids by a truck driver who left her for her sister. Yeah, this Springfield girl I'm building up in my mind sounds like quite a treat. Anyway, look me up, all the same.

**Posted: October 23, 2009 in Springfield, MO**
**Results: 5 Responses, 3 Correspondents, 0 Scrabble Games, and 0 Love**

## Shameless Plug

If you like *My Search For Love On Craigslist*, you might like some other Michael Zinetti creations, available online at michaelzinetti.com. There, you'll find everything there is to know about Michael Zinetti. What he likes to eat. Where he keeps his crayfish catching equipment. And how often he's overcome with fits of irrepressible giggles. Also, you'll be privy to news and links about future writing projects. And did you know? Not only does he write infantile books, he also write infantile songs as well! Currently, he has a cornucopia of songs he's written and recorded, all posted and ready to be downloaded. Someday, they'll be joined by even more songs by his acoustic punk duo, The Michaels. All the hits are currently online, like: "I Could Be A Good Girl," "She Ripped One", "Apple Boobs," "She Impregnated Me," and "Love Is A Mother-Fucker." Thank you for your time, and enjoy the rest of the book!

# 35 Still Awesome, Still Waiting ~ Hub's 5th Attempt

To whom it may concern:

Just because nobody will hire me, doesn't mean I'm not awesome. I can still operate in a very awesome fashion. I will help out. I will help you carry in your groceries, install your printer, and alphabetize your DVD/CD's. When necessary, if all goes well and conditions are at their most optimal awesomeness, I will even have sex with you. So you see, someone doesn't have to have a job to be considered awesome, wouldn't you agree?

More reasons why I'm awesome:

-I can kiss without getting drool on you
-I have most local dollar menus memorized
-Never once has anyone ever complained about me being too big in bed
-I whistle while I work, but I don't work, so you won't have to deal with me whistling all the time
-I rarely belch
-One time I taught a bird to fly
-I'm great at giving back/butt massages
-In the middle of sex, I sometimes get disorientated, and call out my own name
-I can sing like a dying cat
-Sometimes I can comprehend poetry
-I can promise you I will almost always say bless you when you sneeze
-I can get your bra off in seven to ten minutes flat, if you help me
-Last night I dreamed somebody loved me
-I have a way of making people feel valued
-On occasion, I have fallen in love really really fast, I have the restraining orders to prove it
-I can provide references upon request
-My hugs have been known to crack backs
-I went to college and made a real big debt
-I can pee sitting down
-When cornered by old people, I'm polite and listen to their incoherent stories
-I'm starting to like reggae
-Coffee makes me have to poop
-I'm thankful for the men and women serving in our military
-I can play Scrabble really good
-I'm not too cultured
-I won't ask you to peel my grapes for me
-I've only been in two fan clubs, Living Colour and The Bangles, and only once wrote to one of the artists in question requesting nude photos
-When asked to do yard work, I sometimes respond by projectile vomiting

-I tend to have several contradictory political positions, but when it comes time for bed, I only have one position
-I've been guilty of lingering a little too long around the lady handing out samples at the super market
-I have a BA in Creative Writing from MSU, of which I've tried several time to trade for food stamps, to no avail
-When I was a wee lad, I could moonwalk with the best of them
-If you want me to teach you how to catch crayfish I will
-Sometimes I pull a 180 when I only meant to pull a 360
-I've lived in 3 states that start with the word "New"
-I don't discriminate based on race, only poor grammar
-My favorite president would have to be Johnson, I love my Johnson!
-I don't mind letting you be on top

**Posted: October 26, 2009 in Springfield, MO**
**Results: 6 Responses, 0 Correspondents, 0 Scrabble Games, and 0 Love**

## 36 Virgin Seeks To Be Virgin No More ~ Petur's 2nd Attempt

The following is made up:

Looking for small to medium size woman to take my virginity away. Beware! This requires me ejaculating somewhere in the vicinity of you. In which case you may have to touch me. I've had sex before, sure, but this time, I'd really like someone else in the room with me. I've heard it's at least 10 to 20 times better if someone else is there. If you want, I will wear one of those things. However, I have to surmise that my semen is pretty cleanish, given that the only people I've had sex with are bath tissues and cushion cracks and one time my bare hands-that was kinky. This reminds me, I may need you to touch my penis a lot, in order to get it going. In contrast, you may not need to touch it at all, and I may just ejaculate in my pants. If such a thing should occur, I would appreciate it if you didn't laugh or make fun. I think it would show great patience and understanding on your part if you let me use your washer and dryer to clean the semen out of my underwear. While my underwear is getting clean, we could pass the time with a crossword puzzle or Scrabble. It's really up to you. Afterwards, once my underwear is dried, maybe we could try again. If I should ejaculate in my pants again, well, maybe we should take it as a sign that it was never meant to be. If that's okay with you. Out of curiosity, after ejaculating in my pants twice, instead of in or around you, do you think that would pass for losing my virginity? Just wondering...

**Posted: October 30, 2009 in Joplin, MO**
**Results: 1 Response, 0 Correspondents, 0 Scrabble Games, and 0 Love**

## 37 Are You Like Me? ~ Xerx's 6th Attempt

Are you like me? Do you like Scrabble? If so, let's have sex. If you're tired of sitting at home, staring into the abyss that is your love life, because you have no one to play Scrabble with, then look me up and let's have sex.

Are you like me in other ways as well? Are you into cuddling and watching good movies? If so, let's have sex? If you find movie watching a bore, because you know in your heart of hearts your special someone, your one true love is somewhere out there and you feel empty without them, then why don't you stop reading this ad and simply write me and let's have sex.

Also, are you like me? Do you like long walks on the beach? If so, let's find a beach and afterwards, have sex. If you've managed to find the most serene coastal spot on the planet, with a steady soul-soothing tide and a dark blue moonlit sky, but can't quite grasp that elusive sensation of complete and utter contentment because you don't have your soul-mate to share it with, than quick as you can, respond to this ad, and let's have sex.

Finally, and I hate to be so bold, some might even call it obscene, but I would really like to know if you like sex? If so, let's have sex. Are you tired of being in the mood, filled with unquenchable passion and desire, but no outlet to get that satisfying release, since you are condemned to be with a lackluster lover, or worse yet, are alone and forced to improvise with various toys or elongated fruits or vegetables, then by all means, I must insist, spare not even a second, and write me, and let's have sex.

Disclaimer: By sex, I may just mean serious making out, and by serious making out, I may just mean kissing and fondling one another, and by kissing and fondling one another, I may just mean oral sex, and by oral sex, I may just mean putting the whole topic of sex on the backburner to be discussed after we get to know each other, which may entail several dates and several games of Scrabble, at which point it may be determined I am willing to have sex with you, with the understanding that we are in love.

**Posted: November 3, 2009 in Springfield, MO**
**Results: 5 Responses, 3 Correspondents, 0 Scrabble Games, and 0 Love**

# 38 Ode To The Boob ~ Rome's 2nd Attempt

ode to the boob
you boob, you mischievous boob
for the things you do
and for the things you don't do, too

and then your sister (the other boob)
what's up with you two?
up to no good, nothing new
so much bad you make me wanna do

oh, you boob, both of you
together you two collude
and she misconstrues
all that i do

just cuz i tend to stare at you
i see her eyes disapprove
ah, what am i supposed to do?
pretend like you don't protrude?

but wait a minute, you do
both of you!
out you pop, peek-a-boo
so clever, so smooth

it's all some fantastical ruse
to be arranged as you choose
like a pitfall, for the men you would otherwise refuse
or to renegotiate deals with unsuspecting dudes

when you lean over the counter, like you do
then they knock 20% off what's due
i'm onto you, both of you
up to no good, nothing new

it's all true
but i still love you
and i love your sister, too
woe is me and woe is you, too

my how it's difficult to separate the both of you
but it really is something i must do
out of respect for you
and for your sister, too

which one do i choose?

so hard to exclude
but i must pick you
the first one I perused, yeah you
the one on the right, i presume

no, wait a minute, I'm confused
perhaps i drank too much ooze
which one were you?
the one i saw first, my muse?

oh yes, now i conclude
it is you
the mischievous boob
for all along, i knew

and now it is I with the fantastical ruse

you are my favorite boob
for the things you do
and for the things you don't do, too
like making me write this all out for you

my ode to the boob

**Posted: November 6, 2009 in Joplin, MO**
**Results: 2 Responses, 0 Correspondents, 0 Scrabble Games, and 0 Love**

# 39 Manusukling Seeks Earthling Lady From Springfield ~ Petur's 3rd Attempt

The following is made up:

To the earthling ladies of Springfield, I would like to bid a fond hello. My name is Thomas Jefferson, from the planet Manusuk, near Pittsburgh. Anyway, I am a very handsome humanoid creature with lustrous bluish gray skin. Like many of my kind, I am extremely tall and gangly, so my appendages stretch quite far, not unlike my merim - or what humans might equate to a penis. As I've been able to gather, while working in close proximity with humans, when erect, a male earthling's penis averages out to be around 2 korbets or 6 inches. And so, we have deduced that earthling ladies of Springfield are satisfied with this length.

Not so fast!

I recently discovered when given the option between 6 inches and 24 inches, which is the average length of a Manusukling's merim, the earthling ladies of Springfield will choose the 24 inch. I gathered my findings late one night, here on the ship, while the rest of the crew were in a deep sleep state. I crept into the laboratory, where we keep the humans we're studying, and stopped at a particularly pleasant looking female. In the name of science, I carefully dislodged the metallic probing devices from her various orifices, and replaced them with my alien penis. The earthling lady from Springfield, though in a suspended state, smiled almost instantly, and even giggled. I almost aborted the experiment, when, to my sheer horror, the subject suddenly opened her eyes. The earthling, however, was in no way afraid. In fact, she whispered, "Don't stop," and then "Almost there", referring to, I can only presume, an orgasm, of which she had several before the experiment was complete.

Afterwards, we shared a cigarette together. While we smoked, the human went as far as to describe the experience as earth shattering and if she wasn't married, she'd consider returning to Manusuk with me. Then she suggested I try Craigslist, where, as she put it, anybody can find anybody if they're desperate enough. We both shared a laugh, that is, until my alien man-juice, which was nestled deep inside her human vagina, began to give off a burning smell similar to when Manusuklings cook the fanokma meat too long. Perhaps this would be the point of fracture in my hypothesis that Manusuklings might be able to copulate freely with humans. The pain must have been excruciating, because the earthling began to scream uncontrollably. For fear that the others might find out about my extracurricular activities with the humans, in a rather boorish and regrettable fashion, I opened the drop latch and tossed the human overboard, where she and her blood curdling screams steadily faded from sight and sound as she fell to the earth.

On a lighter note, I enjoy snarf sailing, kenubak books, and anime. Please write back soon. I am anxious to continue my experimentation with your kind. Oh, and by the way, I've almost perfected a covering device to keep my alien man juice from burning you alive, which is good.

**Posted: November 24, 2009 in Springfield, IL**
**Results: Flagged and Removed, November 27, 2009**
**Reposted: November 30, 2009 in Springfield, OH**
**Results: Flagged and Removed, December 2, 2009**
**Rereposted: December 11, 2009 in Springfield, MA**
**Results: Flagged and Removed, December 13, 2009**

# 40 Finally Ready To Watch *Children Of The Corn* ~ Michael's 8th Attempt

I'm finally ready to watch *Children of the Corn*. This movie came out when I was a kid and the commercials scared the crap out of me. I don't know what makes it so terrifying, whether it's the corn or it's the children. As far as vegetables go, corn would have to be the creepiest one. Besides maybe Brussels sprouts.

On a side note, what kind of diabolical creepazoid did this guy Brussels have to be to get a vegetable, not to mention the creepiest vegetable ever, named after him? More than likely it's named after the country, Brussels or Belgium, of which is even scarier, given that to this day, and I challenge you to do the same, but I can't think of a single Belgian I've ever trusted. It's also creepy that the vegetable has outlasted its own country, since Brussels doesn't exist anymore. Only the Brussels sprout remains. I bet that never occurred to you, when you saw them sitting there on your plate. Acting almost too innocent. As if the little monsters were privy to some dark secret about the dissolution of its own country. Man, are those shrunken heads of cabbage creepy!

And then there's the matter of children. I don't have to tell you, but everyone knows children are crazy as hell. After clowns, children, as a people, or a movement, or whatever they are, have to be the creepiest sort of things ever invented. I mean, just think of some of the creepy children in your life, or even the famous ones, like that girl from *The Bad Seed*, or Damien, or that little boy from the *Sixth Sense*, that kid is pure evil. Why is he in movies? He creeps me out more than that really f-ed up movie called *Freaks*, from the 20's. Seeing him in that movie *A.I.* sealed the deal for me. I just hope for that kid's sake I never run into him on the streets. Depending on my mood, I might bash his face in, or I might scream like a little girl and run home.

So, no matter what makes *Children of the Corn* scary, whether it's the corn or the children, I finally think I'm ready to see it, but only if you're willing to watch it with me. As a warning, I may need to grab your hand or hide under your sweater while we're watching. For some reason, when it comes to me being scared, breasts seem to be the best calming agent. So be ready for that.

It was great talking. Can't wait to hear from you....

**Posted: November 29, 2009 in Springfield, OH**
**Results: 4 Responses, 2 Correspondents, 0** *Children of the Corn***, and 0 Love**

## 41 Begin Again In Lakewood ~ Davy's 5th Attempt

Sometimes I think about Jamestown, New York. Or more like Lakewood, New York to be exact. I think about how nice it would be to find a sweet girl to settle down with and raise a family in my old neighborhood.

Unfortunately life doesn't always go the way we plan. On the contrary, it seems to go quite the opposite. Perhaps that's the difference between people who make their own destiny and people, like me, who just sort of lay back and let destiny do the driving.

Sometimes I think about people who are progressing, you know, really doing something with their lives, who have careers, great families and whatnot. Why is it that this didn't happen for me? At 35, I sometimes sit there and flip through my friends on Facebook and marvel at how productive their lives have been. I see them posing with their spouses and/or kids and they just look as happy as can be. I check out their occupations, and no matter what it is, it always sounds so impressive, or at least tolerable.

When I was a kid, I used to tell stories. Me and my friend, we'd stay up half the night, telling long and drawn-out stories about our possible futures. The possibilities were virtually limitless. We could try our hand at being rock stars, or baseball players, or just older and somehow cooler. And when things got old, in whatever fictional life we had dreamt up, we'd just say let's start over, and we'd begin again, try something different, and hopefully more exciting, if not more exciting, than just plain different. Sometimes I wish I could do that now. Honestly, a lot of the time, I wish I could do that. Perhaps that's my problem. Maybe that's how I got in this rut in the first place. Perhaps I made the mistake of thinking life is easy come easy go, and if things get awful, I could just start over, just begin again. But, of course, I can't. The life I've lived is pretty much the life I get. And there are no do-overs.

And yet, when I really give my life a good once-over, I think, in the end, I like my life. I haven't married because I haven't found the right one. I haven't had kids cuz I haven't been ready for kids. And I haven't had a blazing career in anything because, well, I didn't want one. I just wanted what I have. I have me. And when that's not enough, I can always write something up, and make it better. In my mind, I can always begin again. And that, to me, is something of a luxury.

Who knows, maybe I'll make it back to Lakewood someday. Or, who knows, maybe I'm already there. After all, the Lakewood I know doesn't really exist anymore. Mapquest will get me to this town called Lakewood, NY, sure, but not the Lakewood I know. That Lakewood only exists in my mind. Mapquest is cool, but not that cool.

**Posted: November 30, 2009 in Chautauqua, NY**
**Reposted: December 29, 2009 in Buffalo, NY**
**Results: 0 Responses, 0 Correspondents, 0 Scrabble Games, and 0 Love**

## 42 I Am Emo Hear Me Roar ~ Emo's 6th Attempt

I'm Emo. I would like to talk to the real live Christian girls in the room. If you are another robot-prostitute please stop reading this ad and move on to the next one. I am Christian so don't even try it. I know all the games you robot-prostitutes play. I'm like *The Matrix*, that way, I'm The One, so I can face a robot-prostitute and win. I put God first. Then boobs second. Sometimes I wonder if God knew what He was doing when He made boobs. Of course He did! He knows everything. He knew that boobs would drive Emo crazy and yet he made girls with boobs anyway. Why would He do that to me? I would like to meet a real live Christian girl. With tons of morals. I would especially like to meet a Christian girl who knows sign language. Emo thinks there's nothing more sexy than a girl who can sign "I love you" or "Fuck me harder." Can you think of anything more sexy? When I meet you, I may fixate on your boobs. For instance, if we're playing Scrabble, and you decide to let your boobs out, there is a very good chance I will probably stare at them. I'm not sure why boobs do this to Emo. If I'm in a room full of modern things like car-parts, bottles, and cutlery, and a pair of boobs, my eyes will almost always gravitate to the pair of boobs. However, if I should see circuitry underneath your boobs, and wires coming out the back, I will absolutely insist you put them back in your shirt. Sure, I might touch them. I might even suck on them. Especially if it's your turn to go and you're taking forever. Emo gets antsy when you take forever to go. Even if I do these things to your robot-prostitute boobs, don't even think for a second it's gonna go anywhere. I'm Christian so don't even try it. You will lose. Anyway, after we have sex, and a week goes by, you better not send me a bill! I won't pay it! Not even if your robot-prostitute pimp comes over and insists that I pay. I am Emo and I have principles. No drugs, no plaster of Paris, no forked tongue beauties, no elves or leprechauns, no venereal diseases, no farm animals, and no paying for sex. If you don't like it, then stop reading this right now. Please be obliged, I am Emo. There are many like me but this one is me. Amen. Counsel your brothers. Let freedom reign. Let the whole world know that today is a day of reckoning.

**Posted: December 3, 2009 in Fayetteville, AR**
**Results: 1 Response, 0 Correspondents, 0 Scrabble Games, and 0 Love**

## **B**onus **A**ttempt: Your Knight In Shining Armor ~ Rome's Attempt

I am your Knight in shining armor. I am your dedicated lover of all things you. I am a ham sandwich when you want cordon bleu. I'll be your fornicator. I am your friend in Scrabble. I am your prison romance. I am your off-brand man. I am your night whisperer of truly sweet nothings, truly. I am your erector set. I am the loud mouth in love with you. I am the wrong number. I am the last train to Clarksville. I am the dragon, hatched and bred in gloom. I am your opposite dream. I will hunt you down with no eye for the season. I am your dinner companion in a restaurant you seldom frequent. I am the essence of negative space. I will give you the things your heart only marginally desires. I am your juxtaposition. I am the silencer who subdues your heart in tumult. I am the knock-down drag-out side of refrain. I am the roller coaster aborted mid-climb. I cry the tears that waterlog the sun. I am the beholder of a majestic you. I am the moth to the third degree burn. I am the pathway to your carnal salvation. I am from whence I came and no more than this. I am your contented conjoined twin. I will bloom the flowers in the back of your mind's eye. I am the front door to your warm safe place. I will still the waters and calm the sea. I am the roar of apnea in the morning of your unrest. I am the kitten misbegotten and five times forgotten. I am the penniless philanthropist in the black. I am the friend you'd rather not fuck. I am your guide to an otherwise good day. I am your suitor clad in split pants. I am the chasm in between your thoughts. I am the granter of untimely wishes. I am your Knight in shining armor, questing for your core. I am what I am, and much much more...

**Honestly, I liked the way this poem was shaping up, but felt it was too good for Rome, and too bizarre for any other persona. This was my orphaned post.**

## 43 Let My Awesomeness Shine On You ~ Hub's 6th Attempt

Is it possible I'm the only awesome person on the planet? I mean, how many girls are reading these ads and just moving on, afraid they're not awesome enough for me? Well…cut it out! Underneath your layers of unawesomeness, maybe there's a tiny bit of awesomeness. Maybe it's down deep where nobody can see it. Maybe it's so tiny, it only surfaces on rare occasions and even then, only someone who's really awesome can see it. Well, don't be discouraged…

I hate to flood you with even more reasons why I'm so awesome, but you probably should know what you're getting yourself into. I believe in full disclosure. And so, here goes….

-I can eat and eat and eat
-I support Obama, still, kinda
-When I go to trivia night at local bars, I can sit and relax and not worry about knowing anything
-I can kiss and grab tit at the exact same time
-I'm open to the idea of polygamy
-If you're gonna send an assassin to kill me, please instruct them to kill me in the beginning of my shift and not at the end, that's just cruel
-I'm not as scared of orcs as I used to be
-I'm immune to moronic reality shows
-One of my shoulders doesn't hurt
-For some unknown reason, I always maintain eye contact with the girls at Hooters
-I pride myself in being broke
-Sometimes I'm sad about the passage of time
-I can ignore you no matter how important you think what you're saying is
-I never could have used a V8
-To me, the word "weird" is a plus, not a minus
-I'm into white girls, Asians, black girls, Hispanic girls, but never at the same time – unless you're into that
-I have no problem watching rated R movies, it's the rated G movies that scare the living poop out of me
-My favorite actor might be Steve Buscemi
-I'm glad when Chuck D and Flavor Flav said, "Fight The Power", they weren't talking about me, since I've never had any power
-I believe in the existence of God, mainly because the alternative is unbearable
-I rarely queef
-Some equality is good, but absolute equality is a George Orwell novel
-I will never limit you sexually, especially if your ambition is to bring one of your girlfriends in on the act
-I'm in an acoustic punk duo called "The Michaels"

-I have all the necessary parts to get you pregnant
-I recently lost money on the stock market
-I haven't once prayed toward Mecca, not on purpose anyway
-I don't need to procreate just to know I exist
-I've given up Dungeons & Dragons, but that doesn't mean I don't keep my characters' sheets in a safe place
-I'm an equal opportunity boob aficionado
-My jeans are clean
-I don't smoke
-Rarely do I give any credence to tradition for the sake of tradition, like showing up with flowers or engaging in foreplay
-I will never bog you down with a giant penis
-I suck at being dishonest
-I fear that my natural habitat may be buffets
-I shy away from being committed, either to a woman or nervous hospitals
-Christmas has no effect on me
-I don't worship idols
-I can be pretty creative, especially if it means getting out of something
-I don't know much, but what I do know, I'm almost certain of
-I'm thoughtful in the way I always allow you extra time to get ready since I'm always late all the time
-I have a strong character, especially when it comes to being consistently undependable
-I'm not intimidated by a woman who works more than me, in fact, I prefer it

**Posted: December 6, 2009 in Springfield, OH**
**Results: 7 Responses, 2 Correspondents, 0 Scrabble Games, and 0 Love**

## 44  Reba McEntire: Trifling Hillbilly Goddess or Grotesque Dragon Lady ~ Michael's 9th Attempt

I can't be the only one grossed out by Reba McEntire. And yet I can't put my finger on why exactly I'm so repelled by her. Possible reasons may be the goofy permanent dumbfounded expression on her face, complete with a very odd muppet-like mouth. Another reason might be her borderline retarded southern dialect, which makes me wanna climb in my pickup, share a mason jar full of moonshine with my cutest cousin, and shoot myself with my momma's shotgun.

The other day I was flipping around the channels and stopped when I heard that unmistakable god-awful voice of Reba McEntire. Just like on 9-11, I was stunned by the sheer horror of what was happening on my TV screen. I guess it was her latest "music" video. She was lying on her bed, with that same old heavy guttural drawl, howling about some boy. I wanted to vomit. Why is this woman still making "music", I thought to myself. She must be like 60 years old, and here she is rolling around in bed like some lovesick teenager. It would have been more fitting if the video consisted of Reba wandering around aimlessly through the aisles of a flea market or dollar store, decked out in her favorite George Strait t-shirt and worn sweat pants, as she leaned against a cart chock-full of discounted goodies, while a swarm of wild grandbabies hooted and hollered all around her.

Anyway, if you, too, live in fear of this horrid dragon lady and need someone to huddle with for protection, in case Reba decides to flap her long black wings over to our town to wreak havoc, then please drop me a line. I like watching movies, playing Scrabble, and avoiding Reba McEntire at all cost.

Other women I'm repelled by for no particular reason: Meryl Streep, Anjelica Huston, Jodi Foster, Glen Close, Jessica Lange, Cate Blanchett, Kathleen Turner, Cher, Chyna Doll, Yoko Ono, Susan Sarandon, Wynonna Judd, Judi Dench, Bette Midler, Geena Davis, Juliette Lewis's retarded way, Scarlett Johansson's voice, and that freakish looking little woman from the new NCIS, Linda Hunt.

**Posted: December 8, 2009 in Tulsa, OK**
**Reposted: December 29, 2009 in Joplin, MO**
**Results: 2 Responses, 0 Correspondents, 0 Scrabble Games, and 0 Love**

# 45 The Decline Of A Scrabble-less Nation ~ Xerx's 7th Attempt

For decades, people have been meeting and falling in love while immersed in a hot and heavy game of Scrabble. Back in the olden days, before there were Hooters girls or premarital sex, there was only Scrabble. Families would gather together and have their children of marrying age play Scrabble with one another until they found the right match. It was a pure and innocent and some might say, better time.

Nowadays, people have their priorities all mixed-up. They will hop into bed with just about anybody, with little regard to whether or not they are Scrabbly-matched. I fear for what might become of a Scrabble-less nation. A land without Scrabble is a sad and destitute land. It is the sort of place goblins shiver and quake over while suffering through yet another sleepless night.

That's why I say bring it back! Return, O nation of wickedness to the way you once were, to a time when young lovers proved their love with a heated game of Scrabble rather than a meaningless blowjob. Honestly, what's so great about a blowjob, especially if you don't know how good or bad the girl giving it is at Scrabble? With Scrabble as a firm foundation, there's very little that can go wrong with a relationship. Find two equally yoked Scrabble players, and I'll show you a happy couple. Anyone can give a blowjob. But can anybody score 200 points on a double triple-word bingo?

This message brought to you by the fine, and somewhat delusional, people at Hasbro, in association with MAB: Mothers Against Blowjobs.

**Posted: December 13, 2009 in Springfield, OH**
**Results: 5 Responses, 3 Correspondents, 0 Scrabble Games, and 0 Love**

## 46 Looking For A Girl Who's Different ~ Petur's 4<sup>th</sup> Attempt

The following is made up:

Looking for a girl who looks nothing at all like me. For once in my life, I would like a girl who's different. So Laurel, Nancy, and Aunt Junifer please don't respond to this here post! I'm not being judgmental. I reckon everyone has their own right to live how they see fit. I just want to find someone different.

Grandpa used to talk about old times, when him and Uncle Uly would go to dances down on the square and meet all kinds of different girls, from town mostly. Sometimes he'd even meet girls from other towns or counties. To hear him tell it, kinda made me excited and sad at the same time. I suppose that's when I first came up with the bright idea to try and find a girl who's different. As far as Grandpa goes, he eventually came to his senses and did the right thing by Grandma, and settled with his kin, as Grandma tells it.

Nobody in our family goes to dances on the square no more. We just keep to ourselves. Grandma says if it's a dance we're itching for, we could clear a space in the barn and Uncle Uly could bring out his fiddle. That's when Laurel and Nancy might get to yipping like wild dogs, on account of how much fun they were gonna have. Sorry, but you aren't gonna see me carrying on that a'way. No offense, Grandma, but that's not good enough for me. Not no more.

I've spent too many nights lying awake in bed, imagining me up a whole new world. Starting with a big ole dancehall down on the square practically lighting up the whole night sky. Next, I come a'walking up, but then I get barreled over by the good-time music pouring out the doors and windows, kinda like the water in the tub, when Aunt Junifer gets in – I'm just funnin'. Anyway, in my dream, I get back up and slap the dust off my trousers and try my best to get my bearings. Only this time, when I hear that sweet sound of the dancehall music, instead of it barreling me over, it's a'calling me, kinda like how Pa used to call the cows to come home, and so I get a move on up the steps and yank on that blessed screen door. And before you can say, "jack rabbit", I'm clear inside. Right in front of me, I spy me a full band, just like Grandpa described, with instruments I never did hear before, not in real life, anyway. And they're playing that good-time music I've only heard on the radio. While I'm listening and a'watching them play their good ole music, I look about the place, and notice all the colorful decorations hanging from the walls and ceiling, right where Grandpa said they'd be. Then, through all the bells and whistles, to my delight, I see a slew of all different kinds of girls, girls I've never seen in all my life, all lined up against the wall and waiting for someone, maybe even me, to ask them to dance. Shoot, I gotta say, real life sure don't measure up to make belief. Ain't that the truth.

Anyway, I reckon I oughta get on with this here ad. So here goes… What I want is a girl who's different. I want a girl who has different colored eyes and different colored hair. I just want someone different. When I feast my eyes on her for the first time, I don't want to know everything about her. Just once, I'd like to take a girl down to Possum Falls and her not know every inch of it, like you, Laurel, or even you, Nancy. I want someone different. I wouldn't care if she was from clear across the county. The more different the better. As long as she is white. I don't think I could date me a colored girl or no Mexican. I just want her to be different. Maybe she can have an interesting feature that sets her apart from the usual, like an accent or a funny birthmark. Things she might have picked up being from a different family and all.

Sometimes I wonder what it would be like if everyone felt this a'way. If folks saw fit to mix up families instead of staying in. I hate to break your heart Laurel, but maybe you can meet someone different, too. You don't have to limit yourself to me or Jacob. You two just don't get along like you could be man and wife. I know he's your brother and all, and you know him like the back of your hand, I just don't see you two being together. Really, Grandma wouldn't judge none. And even if she did, she'd just have to get over it. She's too old fashion for her own good. We're just different, we could tell her. We want something different. She can't keep us forever. It ain't nothing against the family. It's just the way we feel, we could try to tell her.

So you ladies out there, I'd really appreciate it if you dropped me a line. I guess, if you know someone, you could drop Miss Laurel a line as well. She's a good woman, good for cooking and cleaning and a terror in bed. I ain't just saying that because she's my cousin, neither. You couldn't go wrong with her.

Some things I like are television shows, books, and I play a mean game of checkers. Plus, I like swimming at Possum Falls. Sometimes, I pack sandwiches and venture clear down to the edge of the forest, where the Amish live. I get a kick out of watching them and the queer way they get on. They don't mind me watching neither.

Hope to hear from you.

**Posted: December 14, 2009 in Columbus, OH**
**Results: 1 Responses, 1 Correspondents, 0 Scrabble Games, and 0 Love**

## 47 To The Girl I Haven't Yet Met ~ Rome's 3rd Attempt

To the hot hot girl I haven't yet met
Who's really smart and funny and has 2 big ole breasts
With a kind kind heart and angelic smile
One who's moral and just and longs to be sexually defiled

To the cold cold girl I haven't yet met
Who's really strong-willed with a heart never at rest
Yes a sweet sweet girl with a vagina so true
A vagina she bears like a gift but wishes to be abused

To the lukewarm lascivious girl I haven't yet met
Who really digs Scrabble, good music and movies, and giving head
Hear this prayer, O Craigslist gods or devilish things
Or whoever else heeds my words, and with luck she brings

**Posted: December 15, 2009 in Springfield, IL**
**Results: 1 Response, 0 Correspondents, 0 Scrabble Games, and 0 Love**

## 48 Emo Goes To The Girl Factory ~ Emo's 7th Attempt

Once upon a time in Springfield, there was Emo. Emo went to the girl factory and said to the girlmakers, "I'm Emo, hear me roar. I would like a nice Christian girl with tons of morals." The girlmakers nodded, but before they could make his order, Emo stopped them and said real slow, so there wouldn't be any mistakes, "I especially want a human girl with fleshy bubbly human parts with 2 boobs and a wiggle when she walks and giggle when she talks, to make Emo's world go round." The girlmakers nodded again. But even still, Emo was not satisfied, and said, "One moment." The girlmakers looked pissed. "I will not, under any circumstances accept a robot-prostitute girl. No matter how lifelike or perpetually horny she is, she must be a human girl. If I find out, after tons of lovemaking and Scrabble, even after a year has passed, that you tried to pull a fast one on Emo and give him a robot-prostitute, then I will sue you guys for too much money. I'm Christian, so don't even try it!"

Now, when Emo left the Craigslist Girl Factory, he smiled at the girl who sat beside him. She was very beautiful. And she smelled very unmechanical, and Emo liked that. It was Trivia Binge night at the Patton Alley Pub, so Emo decided to bring his brand new girl with him. They joined Emo's usual team, which was called Sofa King Tired Of Losing and settled in with a half-off domestic beer and half-off appetizer. While Emo waited for trivia to commence, Emo looked around for Lionel Richie's Wardrobe, the team who usually kicked everybody's butt too hard. Emo smiled with exceeding glee when they were nowhere to be found. Emo shared this exceeding glee with his brand new special girl, whom he purchased ironically enough on special; giving her so many cute-a-rific glances, their teammates must have known Emo and this girl were truly in love. However, once the trivia started, to Emo's horror, his girl, his brand new girl he ordered special for himself, knew all the answers.

"In light years, approximately how far away is the Andromeda Galaxy from our own?" the Trivia Binge question askers asked.

"2.5 million," Emo's girl said dryly.

Emo's jaw dropped.

"The word 'Presto!' has been used by conjurers for centuries to command unseen demons, and in Italian means 'quickly.' It could have had its start in magic as the shortening of this word that means sleight of hand."

"Prestidigitation," she answered again.

And this went on all night long. While the rest of Emo's team was loving Emo's girl, Emo was loving her not.

During a lengthy round three, also known as the mystery round, the Trivia Binge question askers decided to have a Rock, Paper, Scissors contest. This was an extremely long and drawn out affair, and made Emo sleepy. So he turned to his brand new girl and insisted she join him in the car.

Emo's girl asked, "What's the matter? Would you like to have sex?"
Emo was confused.

Once they were in the car, Emo's girl started taking her clothes off. Her boobs were very boob-like and precious. Emo sat in awe. Then he reached to take hold of them.

"Oh, Emo, that feels good."

Emo smiled. He even laughed to himself. How could he be so stupid? She was no robot-prostitute. She was just smart. Just like he requested from the girlmakers. Anyway, things got hot and heavy and Emo was very happy.

~ fast-forward 2 minutes ~

Emo was trying to find one of his shoes when he heard his girl say, "That will be 200 US Dollars. To be paid directly, cash or credit. Sorry, personal checks not accepted."

Stunned, Emo looked up at her. "I knew it!" Emo screamed like a girl. "I knew you were a robot-prostitute! Nobody knows that much trivia!"

Emo's girl sat by, responding only with a smile as vacant as vacant can be.

"I'm not paying you one red cent!" Emo said. "I'm Christian so don't even try it!" Emo waited for a response.

Then she said, "Emo, darling, why is it, just because I charged you for sex, you assume that I am a robot-prostitute?"

Emo thought about it. Finally, Emo saw through her robot-prostitute ruse. Emo drove directly to the girl factory and demanded to see the girlmaker in charge.

Emo was sitting in the head girlmaker's office. His girl sat beside him.

Finally, some dude came in. Emo thought to dropkick him on sight but decided to wait. The dude sat down at his desk and said, "Sorry to keep you waiting. The girl business is crazy." Then the dude looked at Emo's girl. "I see you know well enough. She is exquisite, isn't she?"

Emo looked at his girl. "Yes."

"So what seems to be the problem, Mr. Emo?"

"Well, frankly, I'm surprised you even have to ask. I'm Emo, first and foremost. And I am Christian. Therefore, I have no use for a robot-prostitute. I would think I made that clear before."

"Yes," the dude said. "I see. That's quite a dilemma."

"Not really, bonehead! Give me my money back! I'm Emo!"

"I'm afraid it's not that simple."

"Why not?"

"We at CGF have a policy. We will not accept returns after consummation. We wouldn't stay in business long if we did. The resale value drops rather significantly after deflowering."

Emo's heart started pumping faster and faster. He wanted to jump up and grab the dude's head and bash it against his desk a couple hundred times. Then maybe hit him. Instead, Emo just sat there. He then thought to say, "Yes. But we didn't actually do anything."

"I would appreciate it if you'd keep your delusions and/or revisionist untruths to yourself. I really am a busy man. I have no time for fantasy."

This made Emo even madder. "I'm not lying! We didn't do anything!"

"Mr. Emo. Our girls are equipped with a pair of LED indication lights when they have been compromised. It shows in their cheeks, to create a faint depiction of rosy cheeks. As you can see, Mr. Emo, your girl has rosy cheeks. And they do make her all the more beautiful, wouldn't you agree, Mr. Emo?"

Emo looked at her. "Yes!" he said, annoyed.

"Is there anything else I can help you with? I really must get back on the floor."

Emo thought about it a minute. "Well, yes. You said you built her. I specifically asked that the girl be human."

"Yes. She is human."

"No she isn't. She's a robot."

"Mr. Emo, what did you think we were going to do? Find you a real live girl? We are a girl factory. Not a whorehouse."

"Well, I should hope not," Emo said, offended by the thought.

"Mr. Emo. She is mostly human. Her skin is fashioned from the finest manmade silken plastics and rubber. It perspires and tans and replenishes itself, just like real skin. I assure you, you will never know the difference. And neither will anybody else. She is as close to the real mccoy as one could be. Now, why don't you take her home and begin your life with her. She will be a very delightful partner for you. We made her extra smart and especially proficient at Scrabble, as you requested. She is configured in such a way that she won't get too bored in church, dwelling on the fact that salvation doesn't pertain to her since she has no soul to give or lose. To make up for this void, she's been given a propensity for shopping, not to mention a slight addiction to collecting useless knickknacks. As I'm sure you've been able to gather, she's been given a rather subdued personality, laced with an unpredictable and completely illogical logarithm, to stay true to the irrational tendencies of the feminine mind. We also gauged her preferences in music and movies according to your likes and dislikes, with some differences to keep things interesting. She will smile and laugh when you are funny. However, simply because you think you're funny, doesn't always mean she will think you're funny, otherwise, you would get very bored, very quickly. She will enjoy cuddling with you. And she will rub your back when you need it. In front of others, she will side with you, even when you are wrong. However, when it is just the two of you, she will simply state gently when you are wrong. And all of this is just the tip of the iceberg. So tell me, Mr. Emo, with all that said, what more could you ask for?"

Emo nodded. He looked again at the girl. The head girlmaker was pretty right. She was very beautiful and life-like. And you could hardly tell that she was a robot. Then Emo said, "What about this prostitution thing? Where do you get off giving me a girl that's gonna charge me every time we have sex?"

The dude leaned back in his chair. He smiled at the girl. The girl smiled back at the dude. Emo noticed this. "Mr. Emo, what you got there is the finest robot-prostitute money can buy. I'm sure it was worth whatever she charged you."

"No way! She charged me 200 bucks!"

"I believe that is the going rate."

Emo suddenly stood up. "No way! I don't have that kind of money! I need a girl who isn't gonna charge me! I'm a Christian! I don't like prostitutes."

"Yes," he said. "Well, why don't you give her the 200 US Dollars, as she requested, and I'll see what we can do. Next time, I suggest you negotiate a price you're both happy with before you proceed."

Emo stood up! "I told you, doc! I'm Christian! I will not pay for sex!!!"

"Relax, Mr. Emo. Some of our best customers are Christians. Now, will you please sit down?"

Emo remained standing, glaring at the head girlmaker.

As they looked at each other for an extended silence, Emo's girl suddenly said, "I'm sorry I charged you 200 US Dollars. Perhaps, I will permit you to mount me once more, free of charge."

Emo's eyebrows rose. As did the head girlmaker's. Emo glanced back at her. She was smiling.

Then Emo said, "Maybe this'll work out after all."

"Yes, indeed," the head girlmaker said.

Emo took his brand new girl by the hand and said to the dude, just to make sure, "Did you say some of your best customers are Christians?"

"That's precisely what I said."

"And earlier. About her soul?"

"What about her soul, Mr. Emo?"

"Did you say she doesn't have one?"

"As far as I know, Mr. Emo, we haven't yet perfected the whole soul making thing. Just the girl part. But I'll tell you what, if we happen to stumble on how to make a soul, you just bring your girl in and we'll be happy to give her one, free of charge."

"Wow. That's great. I'm sure glad we got this all worked out."

"Me too, Mr. Emo."

"Now if you'll excuse me," Emo said, all proud, "I have a free ride on the robot-prostitute roller coaster coming to me."

**Posted: December 16, 2009 in Springfield, OH**
**Results: 6 Responses, 1 Correspondents, 0 Scrabble Games, and 0 Love**

# 49 Is There Anybody Out There? ~ Bane's 6th Attempt

Is there anybody out there? When my therapist said I should try Craigslist, I have to tell you I was pretty skeptical. But now I know I was right to be skeptical. Cuz it's been a disaster. It's been so bad I'm thinking, if this ad doesn't work, I'm gonna join a monastery. And who knows, maybe I will...

All I'm asking for now is a girl under 6 foot, with hair of any color or length, who has shape to her, meaning any evidence of puberty will do. She can be in a cult, smoke, have a record, have tattoos, belch incessantly, and have a speech impediment. I just don't care anymore. She can do drugs, have 10 kids, currently live with her ex-boyfriend, fart for attention, drink socially and antisocially, and harvest skin in a Petri dish. I don't care! A couple months ago, I was after a girl who likes Scrabble or Boggle, but now I'll just take a girl who can read at a third grade level, if not, than at least be able to spell or recognize her own name. I used to be crazy and insist on a girl who likes sex, especially nasty crazy stuff, but now I'll be happy with a girl who's mildly afraid of it, or equates it to taxes, done once a year, and even then reluctantly. In one post, I even said I'd like a left-handed girl so she can grab my Johnson more easily while I'm driving. Now I'll be happy if she doesn't even have hands. Who knows, maybe a hook or prosthetic hand would feel just as good. I might even start to like it. Just like I might start to like a girl who goes to a super happy no-consequences, no-rules church, who's hymnals are chock full of songs about sunshine and flowers instead of, oh I don't know, salvation. Just a girl, one who doesn't burst into flames whenever she goes to church, would be fine at this point. Speaking of bursting into flames, I don't care if she is a vampire, werewolf, bank robber, alien, illegal alien, or a ninja. It just doesn't matter anymore. Admittedly, I used to get hung up on the details. Now I say, who cares! Just get your jiggly, pimply, discolored, splotchy, hairy, tattooed, patchy, cakey, gangrene, wrinkly, aromatic, black and blue ass over here! Bane is lonely!!!

**Posted: December 18, 2009 in Springfield, IL**
**Results: 5 Responses, 0 Correspondents, 0 Scrabble Games, and 0 Love**

# Adieu

For the love of Scrabble, I'm finished! 50 personals ads posted on Craigslist! I did it! And you were right there with me, every step of the way. Now, I just need to tally the results and see which personae/attempts were the most successful.

You might have noticed a while back, I started posting the ads outside of Missouri. This is because I started seeing someone and although she was good enough to let me finish this project, given I had already spent eight months and written forty ads for it, her lone condition was I had to post the ads outside of Missouri, which didn't really screw things up too much. After forty times around on this merry-go-round, I could pretty much tell when correspondences might advance to the Scrabble stage. At which point, I had to come clean about this whole thing. To their credit, those women were always understanding of the situation. In some cases even anxious to know when the book would be coming out, so they might be able to buy a copy! Oh, by the way, oddly enough, I didn't meet my girlfriend through one of these ads…but by trolling for olives, ours is a different sort of affair.

Anyone who bought this book, thank you very much! I appreciate the support! To anyone who might have found one of my ads on Craigslist, no matter if you merely read the ad and clicked out or if you responded and we actually met and dabbled in a bit of Scrabble, I thank you for your time and I'm sorry things didn't work out. In all sincerity, I hope your search for love, wherever it may take you, proves fruitful.

God bless and happy Scrabbling!

# 50 Need A Girl For Churching ~ Michael's 10th Attempt

I need a girl for churching. Don't get me wrong. I love church as much as the next guy. If it weren't for all the nodding off and general self-loathing it causes, I think it would rank up there with going to Hooters or heading over to the pub for some trivia bingeing. As it stands, and let me tell you -there's far too much of that as well- church is just way too boring. That's where you come in. We will meet for church:

However, before the actual church portion of this affair, we need something to silence our grumbling stomachs. So, first off, we'll meet for breakfast at McDonalds and get all filled up with salty, fatty foods and turn our little temples into murky swamp-flooded theme parks, where all the rides have slowed to stop and will no longer run.

Then, after we've procrastinated as long as we can, getting to know each other with charming conversation and awkward laughs and everything, we'll make our way over to the church.

During the singing portion of church, we'll try to stand up as long as everyone else, but when we feel our legs about to give, we'll lean on each other for support. We can pretend it's like a game. But, no matter what, no matter how numb our legs are, we can't sit down. If we do, everyone will think we're less Christiany than them. Or worse yet, they'll think sometime between last Sunday and this Sunday, we lost our salvation and now we're god-awful heathens come to suck their blood. And let me tell you, when they look at you like that, it's no kind of fun. Take it from one who knows. When the song leader(s), you know, the loudmouths with the permanent clownish smiles on their faces, feel we've suffered long enough, they'll say something like, "please be seated". But in reality, you'll realize they actually said, "Praise God" and now they've started another song you've never heard of and they're gonna sing it twenty times over. Around this time, you'll look at me with nothing but hate. I'll try to smile, as I rub my legs, trying to get the feeling back in them.

Next, we'll have to listen to like a million innocuous announcements. It'll be loads of useless info in various forms, so make sure and listen. They'll tell us about various things and general counsel meetings and whatnot, including votes and minutia like that -you know the kind of stuff God just eats up during all his celestial board meetings in heaven.

After this, the dude that's been sitting there this whole time will stand up. This is the preacher. This is the part where I'll need you most. Sometimes the preacher manages to deliver a pretty good sermon. This is about 10% to 15% of the time. In which case, we might be able to listen. However, for the most part, it'll be pure torture, mixed in with a couple cute anecdotes. The anecdotes are like occasional glimpses of dry land, as we stare through the fog on a rickety barge drifting along on shark-infested waters with seemingly no hope of finding shore.

Sometimes, when I've had enough coffee, I get the notion to follow along in the Bible, but the preacher flips from passage to passage so fast, I usually give up by the third or fourth passage. In no time, we'll be completely lost in whatever the preacher's saying.

To pass the time, we might start people-watching. I might point out some equally lost dude in a suit and tell you he's a money-hungry buffoon who will make sure and tell you how much money he makes within the first 30 seconds of meeting him. Then I might point out some couple and tell you the woman is more than likely having an affair with one of the deacons. You know, just about anything to keep us from falling asleep.

If we feel the inclination, we might want to hold hands during this part. You know, and feel like we're suffering through all this God-awful church like it's our lot in life. I might whisper something like, "I wish I had a pony, on a boat, out on the ocean." And if I'm lucky, you'll say, "I love Lyle Lovett."

Next, we can take out whatever's in our pockets. I'll show you my movie pass to "Up In The Air" and tell you it was pretty good. I'll also flip through my car keys, wallet, some loose change, a guitar pick, and a pack of gum. You'll ask for a piece. I'll give it to you. Then you'll take everything out of your pocket book. You'll have a cell phone, a package of Kleenex, some credit cards, and your license. At which point, we might commiserate over our unfortunate pictures on our licenses. Then you'll go back to going through your stuff. Like some change, some money folded up, and lastly, a condom meant for your ex-boyfriend, who you would sooner see given a lethal injection than in any other capacity.

Naturally, my eyes will focus on the condom. You'll seem to discover it for the first time, and grab it and shove it back into your pocketbook, before looking straight ahead at the preacher, who is prattling on and on about promiscuous sex of all things. I'll notice that you missed your pocketbook, and the condom fell to the carpet, and rolled, ever curiously, under the chair in front of us, where it now rests up against some dude's black dress shoes. In an act of chivalry, if nothing else, I'll lean down and try to grab it for you. Then you'll realize what I'm doing. You'll see it too and start to freak out. You'll slip out of your pumps and try to get your toe on it and drag it back over. No luck.

Then, in an effort to pass more time, I'll smile whimsically and suddenly pull you down onto the not so soft carpet. Then I'll grab the condom and struggle to get it on. You'll look at me, then at it, then me, then at it again. Then you'll shrug your shoulder and like magic, slip off your panties. Then you'll lay me down and get on top.

Then, out of nowhere, some lady will suddenly scream her head off and stand up and point, unable to formulate a coherent sentence. The woman's shrill shout of terror will wake the congregation up from their sermon-induced comas. Then everyone else will stand up. More women will scream. The children will have already been dismissed for Sunday School, so thank God for that. The congregation will join in on a collective bout of shock, gasping in sheer horror. The preacher will try to see over the pulpit, but like usual, he doesn't know what's going on.

For fear that my elbows might chafe on the coarse carpet, not to mention your knees, as you ride me, I'll carefully turn you over, trying my best not to slip out. Once I've got you underneath me, I'll grip your round fleshy butt (let's be honest, we've all let ourselves go a bit –nothing to be ashamed of), and slowly start easing myself inside and out. You might smile, as you feel the stirring sensations collecting around your insides, as you close your eyes and arch your head back and open your eyes and look upside down at the people watching.

Meanwhile, the deacons will start to clear everyone out, shielding the women's eyes, as if they'd never seen two people screwing on the sanctuary floor. The preacher, a bit dejected by the interruption, almost certain he was finally getting a handle on his sermon, and was about to bring it all together, will close the Bible and reluctantly shuffle out after his flock.

Seemingly unaware of the fact that we're all alone now, if you're particularly sacrilegious, you might say, "Oh my God," as you feel yourself nearing the mountaintop. Right about then, after hearing His name, God might come down off the cross on the wall, and pause in front of us, shaking His head. At which point, I might get all star-struck and reach over for a Bible and ask Him for His autograph, all the while, keeping a steady pace on you. Maybe He will, maybe He won't. Either way, I'll make a fist, and shout, "Right on, Jesus!" Then He will see that I do love Him after all and sign my Bible with His blood. As soon as Jesus has left the building, right away, I'll start fantasizing about the kind of money an innocent blood-signed Bible from God Himself would fetch on Ebay! I'll get so excited, I think I might finish, but that's when all my excitement will suddenly be dwarfed by how excited you get, when you finally reach the mountaintop, yourself. I ride the wave of your convulsing body, suddenly inspired to try and get you another one.

Before I can even set my sights on this endeavor, if I know my luck, the police would probably show up. And yeah, I'd be a little pissed. Right away, I'll start telling them about how I haven't finished yet. I'd probably go on and on about how I can't feel anything with these damned condoms on. One of them will know what I'm talking about and nod. The other one, the no-nonsense one won't seem to care and grab me -the bastard. Then we'll be handcuffed and escorted out of the church.

When we get outside, the congregation will be huddled about on the lawn like school kids during a fire drill, wondering when they have to go back in, half hoping they don't have to go in at all. Somebody might shout, "Shame on you!" One of the deacons, the gallivanting one, will wish he got a pic of you when your dress started to fall off your shoulder, exposing half a tit. So will I, for that matter. One of the more fervent Christiany folks might jump at the chance to march right up to us and inform us we are no longer welcome at their church. I might feel bad. Then again, I might smile, remembering there's like a million other churches in this God-awful town. Ultimately, I'm not sure how I'd feel.

Then we'll be put in separate cruisers. I'll only see you in passing at the police station. The few times we see each other, we'll probably make faces at each other, like we're common riff-raff up to no good. At some point, we'll be booked for indecent exposure and lewd behavior. While we're waiting, we'll have to sit in a jail cell with the real criminals. We'll keep to ourselves, careful not to piss anybody off. Finally, after booking, we'll be sent home without any supper.

I like to think as we're leaving, we might exchange contact info in front of the courthouse, so we can make plans to try another church next week. If we're feeling at all frisky, and the mood's just right, we'll kiss each other goodbye.

Besides churching, I also like Scrabble, going to movies, and cuddling. For the record, I'm not interested in a no-strings-attached relationship. A Christian non-smoker would be ideal, but in today's America, one must keep an open mind.

**Never Posted For Fear I'd Be Struck By Lighting. Instead, I Published It Here, Where Nobody Would Ever See It...**

# Index

**Pauses**

Dedication, p.3
Some Ground Rules, p.4
Personae, p.9
Greetings, p.14

Shameless Plug, p.57
Adieu, p.82
Index, p.87
Tally, p.89

**Michael: 10 Attempts**

Intro, 5
1 In Search of Scrabble and/or Movie Buddy ~ 1st Attempt, p.6
2 I Guess Nobody Likes Scrabble ~ 2nd Attempt, p.7
3 Scrabble Addict Seeks Hot Brainy Girl To Scrabble With ~ 3rd Attempt, p.8
8 Where Is Joplin Anyway? ~ 4th Attempt, p.20
Bonus Attempt: In Search Of A Sancho-Like Girl, p.23
15 Any Scrabble Lovers In Springfield? ~ 5th Attempt, p.32
22 Wanna Go To The Movies? ~ 6th Attempt, p.41
30 Looking For A Model ~ 7th Attempt, p.50
40 Finally Ready To Watch *Children Of The Corn* ~ 8th Attempt, p.66
44 Reba McEntire: Trifling Hillbilly Goddess or Grotesque Dragon Lady ~ 9th Attempt, p.72
50 Need A Girl For Churching, 10th Attempt, p.83

**Xerx: 7 Attempts**

Intro, p.10
4 Scrabble/Sex Addict Seeks Hot Sugar-Momma ~ 1st Attempt, p.11
10 Sex/Scrabble EXPLOSION! ~ 2nd Attempt, p.22
17 Hooters/Scrabble Fantasy ~ 3rd Attempt, p.34
24 Scrabble/G-Spot Adventuring Party ~ 4th Attempt, p.43
26 Looking For A Girl To… ~ 5th Attempt, p.45
37 Are You Like Me? ~ 6th Attempt, p.61
45 The Decline Of A Scrabble-less Nation ~ 7th Attempt, p.73

**Emo: 7 Attempts**

Intro, p.12
5 Would You Like To Meet Up? ~ 1st Attempt, p.13
9 Would You Like To Meet (Please Humans Only)? ~ 2nd Attempt, p.21
16 Where Are You MelissaXXX? ~ 3rd Attempt, p.33
25 Life After MelissaXXX ~ 4th Attempt, p.44
32 Church Girl Needed For Mexican Food ~ 5th Attempt, p.53
42 I Am Emo Hear Me Roar ~ 6th Attempt, p.68
48 Emo Goes To The Girl Factory ~ 7th Attempt, p.77

**Hub: 6 Attempts**

Intro, p.15
6 Awesome Guy Seeks Awesome Girl ~ 1st Attempt, p.16
12 Still Awesome And Still Looking ~ 2nd Attempt, p.26
20 More Reasons Why I'm Awesome ~ 3rd Attempt, p.38
27 You Want Me So Bad It Hurts ~ 4th Attempt, p.46
35 Still Awesome, Still Waiting ~ 5th Attempt, p.58
43 Let My Awesomeness Shine On You ~ 6th Attempt, p.70

**Davy: 5 Attempts**

Intro, p.18
7 This Probably Won't Work ~ 1st Attempt, p.19
11 Looking For A Girl Who's Okay With The Following ~ 2nd Attempt, p.24
18 A Nice Christian Nymphomaniac Girl ~ 3rd Attempt, p.35
28 Who Wants To Cuddle? ~ 4th Attempt, p.48
41 Begin Again In Lakewood ~ 5th Attempt, p.67

**Truck: 2 Attempts**

Intro, p.28
13 Serious In Need ~ 1st Attempt, p.29
19 Girl Boobs (Chinese) ~ 2nd Attempt, p.36
Truck Dilemma, p.37

**Bane: 6 Attempts**

Intro, p.30
14 Looking For The Right Girl ~ 1st Attempt, p.31
21 Revised Wants And Needs ~ 2nd Attempt, p.40
23 Seriously Loosening Up On Qualifications ~ 3rd Attempt, p.42
29 In Need Of Girl With 2 Boobs ~ 4th Attempt, p.49
33 Still Looking And Yet Not Finding The Perfect Girl ~ 5th Attempt, p.54
49 Is There Anybody Out There? ~ 6th Attempt ~ p.81

**Rome: 3 Attempts**

Intro, p.51
31 To My Sweet Craigslist Princess (Or Something Like That) ~ 1st Att., p.52
38 Ode To The Boob ~ 2nd Attempt, p.62
Bonus Attempt: Your Knight In Shining Armor, p.69
47 To The Girl I Haven't Yet Met ~ 3rd Attempt, p.76

**Petur: 4 Attempts**

Intro, p.55
34 Famous Cowboy In Town For One Night Only ~ 1st Attempt, p.56
36 Virgin Seeks To Be Virgin No More ~ 2nd Attempt, p.60
39 Manusukling Seeks Earthling Lady From Springfield ~ 3rd Attempt, p.64
46 Looking For A Girl Who's Different ~ 4th Attempt, p.74

# Tally

This is a loose, highly nonscientific estimation to try and determine which persona was the most effective, given the amount of attempts, responses, correspondences, games of Scrabble, etc. Oh, and I almost forgot; most love.

**1st Place ~ Michael, 11 Attempts (9 Posted)**
Tally: 40 Responses, 18 Correspondents, 8 Scrabble/Movies/Shoots, and 0 Love
Avg.: 4.4 Responses, 2 Correspondents, .8 Scrabble/Movie/Shoots, and 0 Love
Best: 15 Any Scrabble Lovers In Springfield? 5th Attempt, p.32

**2nd Place ~ Xerx, 7 Attempts**
Tally: 19 Responses, 11 Correspondents, 2 Scrabble, and 0 Love
Avg.: 2.7 Responses, 1.6 Correspondents, .28 Scrabble, and 0 Love
Best: 26 Looking For A Girl To… ~ 5th Attempt, p.45

**3rd Place ~ Davy, 5 Attempts**
Tally: 18 Responses, 6 Correspondents, 2 Scrabble, and 0 Love
Avg.: 3.6 Reponses, 1.2 Correspondents, .4 Scrabble, and 0 Love
Best: 18 A Nice Christian Nymphomaniac Girl ~ 3rd Attempt, p.35

**4th Place ~ Hub, 6 Attempts**
Tally: 34 Responses, 9 Correspondents, 0 Scrabble, and 0 Love
Avg.: 5.6 Responses, 1.5 Correspondents, 0 Scrabble, and 0 Love
Best: 12 Still Awesome And Still Looking ~ 2nd Attempt, p.26

**5th Place ~ Emo, 7 Attempts**
Tally: 21 Responses, 4 Correspondents, 1 Sancho, and 0 Love
Avg: 3 Responses, .57 Correspondents, .14 Scrabble/Sancho, and 0 Love
Best: 32 Church Girl Needed For Mexican Food ~ 5th Attempt, p.53

**6th Place ~ Bane, 6 Attempts**
Tally: 16 Responses, 5 Correspondents, 0 Scrabble, and 0 Love
Avg.: 2.6 Responses, .8 Correspondents, 0 Scrabble, and 0 Love
Best: 23 Seriously Loosening Up On Qualifications ~ 3rd Attempt, p.42

**7th Place ~ Petur, 4 Attempts**
Tally: 7 Responses, 4 Correspondents, 0 Scrabble, and 0 Love
Avg.: 1.7 Responses, 1 Correspondent, 0 Scrabble, and 0 Love
Best: 34 Famous Cowboy In Town For One Night Only ~ 1st Attempt, p.56

**8th Place ~ Rome, 4 Attempts (3 Posted)**
Tally: 4 Responses, 1 Correspondents, 0 Scrabble Games, and 0 Love
Avg.: 1.3 Responses, .3 Correspondents, 0 Scrabble, and 0 Love
Best: 31 To My Sweet Craigslist Princess (Or Something Like That) ~ 1st Attempt, p.52

**9th Place ~ Truck, 2 Attempts**
Tally: 0 Responses, 0 Correspondents, 0 Scrabble Games, and 0 Love
Avg.: 0 Responses, 0 Correspondents, 0 Scrabble Games, and 0 Love
Best: Both equally horrific

Made in the USA
Charleston, SC
02 February 2011